I like...the lively, concentrated and comprehensive way you throw open a series of doors to a new life...I share your feelings that the purpose of therapy is to facilitate a growth and development trip...

Joseph B. Wheelwright, M.D.

Margaret Frings Keyes

THE INWARD JOURNEY

Art as Psychotherapy for You

Photographs by Michelle Vignes

CELESTIAL ARTS
MILLBRAE, CALIFORNIA

First Printing, September 1974
Second Printing, January 1975
Library of Congress Card No.: 74-10122
ISBN: 0-912310-83-9
Made in the United States of America

Library of Congress Cataloging in Publication Data

Keyes, Margaret Frings, 1929—
        The inward journey.

        1. Art therapy.   2. Transactional analysis.
3. Gestalt therapy.   4. Psychoanalysis.   I. Title.
RC489.A7K48   616.8'916'5   74—10070
ISBN 0—912310—81—2

PREFACE

The nineteen-sixties saw a surge in the development of group therapies and techniques—for several reasons: Group treatment provided the patient a financial economy. Group treatment made it possible for more people to be treated effectively by one therapist (or several co-therapists). But most importantly, group treatment provided an effective shortcut for the treatment of a wide variety of emotional, behavioral and marital problems.

Prior to the nineteen-sixties the small amount of group therapy that was practiced derived its model largely from classical analytic thought; the group, by some, was seen as having a personality of its own; or, members of the group were treated on an individual basis; or they engaged in a social interaction that for many was helpful but for others was less than therapeutic.

Only after group therapists began to make use of the insights and techniques developed by Eric Berne (Transactional Analysis) and Fritz Perls (Gestalt Therapy) and others of their followers did group therapy have the potential to become a treatment modality in which profound and lasting change could be effected in a relatively short period of time. (The development of this potential depended to a great degree upon the training and skill of the therapist.)

Margaret Keyes has a rich background in both individual and group therapy. Her personal work with Eric Berne and Fritz Perls, her training in Jungian Psychology, her experiences in artistic exploration and her sensitivity as a therapist have all brought her to a point where she is now able to offer us a clear and helpful synthesis. The use of graphic and plastic techniques coupled with verbal and nonverbal exercises specifically designed to bring feelings and conflicts into consciousness can accelerate and improve the therapeutic process. In *The Inward Journey* Margaret Keyes has given all of us— patients, therapists, students and the general public—an exciting gift to help each one of us on our own inward journey.

William M. Lamers, Jr., M.D.

CONTENTS

vi

ACKNOWLEDGEMENTS

In the course of writing this book I have received encouragement and immeasureable assistance from critical comments on the initial draft by Joseph Wheelwright, M.D., and his wife, Jane Wheelwright, Jungian analysts, from Joel Latner, Ph.D., Gestalt therapist and from Mary Goulding, M.S.W., transactional analyst. My greatest debt, of course, is to the men with whom I studied, Fritz Perls and Eric Berne, whose theory has shaped so much of my current practice.

This book is based on the experience of actual people, clients and group participants who have shared their lives with me. To them, to my friend and photographer Michelle Vignes and to my husband Vincent Keyes who insisted I write the book, I can not sufficiently express my gratitude.

The illustrations and descriptive comments are from my clients and workshop participants and used with their permission.

Margaret Frings Keyes

THE INWARD JOURNEY

Art as Psychotherapy
for You

INTRODUCTION

ART AND PSYCHOTHERAPY

Men have always used the arts of music, poetry, dance, drama, painting, writing, and sculpture to symbolize, explore, and say what could not be said in words. The creative genius of other men's works illuminates the individual's situation, mirrors and deepens his questions. As a therapist, I can select and relate creative works to my client's condition to the degree I know the rewards in these forms—art can open directions for him to pursue. My concern here is to describe in practical detail how I use art materials with the nonartist, the client who has come into therapy with some very specific questions and problems. Some of these questions are similar to your own for they are the questions of anyone who seeks to understand himself, his thoughts, his feelings and actions.

1

These art processes, originally developed in work with troubled clients, I have used in workshops with teachers, students, ministers, and a range of people who simply wished to know themselves more deeply and who found these methods useful. This book is written for you to share these means and utilize them for your own self-growth.

A crisis is usually the precipitating agent to psychotherapy. Paradoxically, it is the unwanted divorce, the loss of a goal, the recognition of incapacity or inner emptiness, boredom or restlessness which opens the way to new growth by finally forcing a symbolic clearing of ground and pruning of dead forms. Men who have found that competition and achievement only lead to more of the same with diminishing flavor, women whose roles are changing before their eyes and who can no longer feel settled down in marriage and motherhood—realistically, the first step for them is to look at where they are.

In the treatment situation, this is done either individually or in a small group of people about the same age but with varying life circumstances. Although I work individually in a number of different ways, when the situation allows I prefer to start with a week of intensive treatment in which the client comes every day and works for whatever period of time something meaningful is happening.

This is a time of clearing away old self-images like unfinished business from the past with parents or spouse. It is a time of identifying recurring patterns of behavior and looking at the underlying questions they have been attempting to answer. And, it is a time of looking at how an individual now perceives himself—the changing body image, varying energy levels, specific talents, interests that may have been laid aside, training that may or may not be worth bringing up-to-date in terms of the person he now feels himself to be.

This first week characteristically releases a significant increase of energy and subjective feeling of well-being and self-value. Undoubtedly this is partially due to the repressed parts

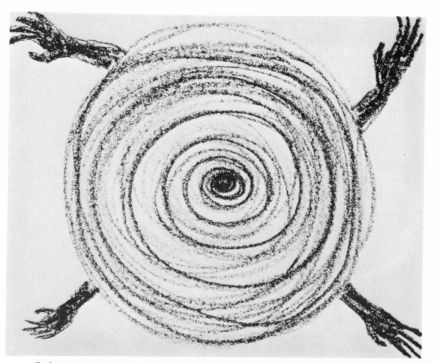

I drew a picture of my fear. It seems to be a vortex with hands reaching out to pull me in.

being listened to and taken seriously, but also because the process itself brings an upwelling of forgotten memories, and the sense of self grows fuller as the roots and connections are seen.

There is no set way to begin treatment. In my practice, I often use videotape, initially setting the camera for a full body view and letting the client tell his story without interruption or comment. When he has finished we replay the tape and reset the camera for a close-up of his face as we discuss what he has seen. This too is replayed and allows the client to experience direct body data for the first time: the expressive use of his eyes and mouth, his style of interaction, his aggressiveness or hesitancy, his need to explain, or sometimes his lack of hearing, the areas of tension in his body and voice. Most people program their behavior and communication in terms of how they expect to be perceived. They modify behavior in terms of interactional cues, e.g., I see you wince when my voice is too loud, I tone down my voice and become more aware of my own excitement because I see your reaction.

The client, via the videotape, has access to direct information about himself that is not ordinarily available to him. This awareness itself causes a process of change. For example, Addie had remarkable physical beauty but a tight, querulous voice and an expression that went with it. They clearly did not fit her body. As we viewed the tape, she said she sounded and looked like her mother—her mother was very uncertain of her own value and place with her husband, a woman who had her daughter's teeth capped and nose bobbed, constantly talked to Addie about how fat she was, and who also gave and withheld gifts from her.

The therapy questions now became "Why was Addie still carrying her parent in her body?" and "What did this have to do with her difficulty?" She had periods of being unproductive in her profession during which she would gain huge amounts of weight. Such obvious and vivid feedback revealed an image of the parent which had been taken inside and it felt like Addie herself. This does not happen often but the client always sees some aspect of his behavior in a different light.

Art therapy does not answer the questions. It provides a process to clarify and deepen the questions, an awareness of how the individual here and now participates in creating his life conditions, and it points to some options that might be chosen. There are no highly visible models for this task. It is an individual journey. The individual has to take back parts of himself which he dislikes and does not want to see. He has to differentiate his own path from the ways of unthinking conformity to *what is done by most people.* He has to discover his own dark and negative side and the elements in his personality that are like those of the opposite sex. In order to make this discovery a family sculpture, a journal of dreams, beginning dialogue work, and Gestalt psychodrama will carry the process forward.

Art materials vivify the process and reach different levels of the personality than can words alone. Clay is used for its sensory, tactile qualities and capacity to bring out the as yet unworded. I particularly like to use it when I have someone who stays away from his feelings by analyzing and speculating on the *whys* of his behavior. In one instance I brought in a married couple for a completely nonverbal session. A partition was placed between them and each worked with clay to depict what their relationship felt like, then the relation to the most problematic parent for each, and finally to their child. At this session, looking at her husband's sculpture of a wall separating her from him and their son, the wife recognized how deeply her husband identified with their mentally defective son who had been placed in foster care immediately after infancy. The mother felt his care was too burdensome to her own career, and her husband felt he too was expendable to her driving ambition! As they talked she began to understand how much her ambition was a cover for her own feelings of vulnerability which were rooted in a reaction to the *helplessness* of her mother.

Clay is useful in the exploration of sticky, messy, bad feelings. Bob, a young doctor, used clay to smear and skin-print portions of his journal as he described and almost embodied his self-disgust, his anger, and his confusion about his need for love and approval which prevented him from showing other people either his anger or his strength. His treatment was complex as was his use of art materials. He used music and movement to express different kinds of feelings warring within him. Some of it was terrifying. He created two foam rubber sculptures—Good Mother and Bad Mother—one, soft and lovely, the other with wild eyes, a jagged mouth, and bloody vagina. At one point he jumped up, bit off her nipples, ripped a knife from his pocket and plunged it repeatedly into her body until he collapsed crying and sobbing with his arms around Good Mother. This session marked a turning point in treatment and in his relationship to me. He had previously been unable to express negative feelings towards his own mother or towards me. We were now able to talk about them and he had a series of psychodrama confrontations with his mother going back to different ages, telling her what he resented and how he was hurting. With role reversal (in which he acted and expressed the thoughts and feelings of his mother) he was able to reach some differentiation of his fantasies from what her reality may have been. With the inner dialogues (written conversations with characters from his dreams) and psychodrama exercises, he came to recognize the positive and negative female aspects in his own personality and the expressive needs these represented.

Inner dialogues are written when the client recognizes a dream character or element which behaves in a significant way in one or more dreams. He addresses several questions to the character and imagines the other's responses, in effect writing a dialogue much as in a play. This is useful; he gets in touch with knowledge he has but did not recognize. In psychodrama, the client describes a scene to me, either an actual past event (when Bob was eight years old, his father brought him a surprise, a horse; Bob was terrified and his father, angry and disgusted, called him a girl) or an anticipated encounter (Bob was planning to apply for a bank loan and anticipated feeling vulnerable and defensive). We imagine the stage and set it with what props are necessary in chairs and space and the client and I act it out. He plays each part and I change places with him becoming whatever other person is needed. We then act alternative ways of doing the same scene, sometimes just giving voice to the feelings and thoughts which had previously been unspoken. His understanding and control deepens as he recognizes emotionally more aspects of each situation, options for his future choices, and ways of saying goodbye and finishing situations with which he was burdened in the past.

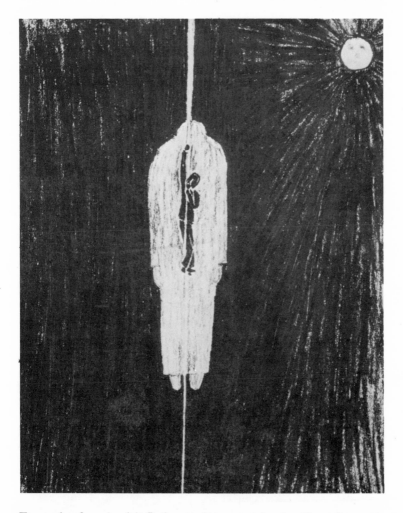

Example of work with fiction to deepen understanding of aspects of self: *I have just read Charles Williams' novel DESCENT INTO HELL. This represents the two central characters—one man committed suicide yet found redemption through love. The other man climbs down a rope into hell with a self-centered love that becomes monstrous. They represent possible choices I see but have not looked at before.*

Psychotherapy to be effective has to provide a means for knowing and understanding both the world we have built and our activity in creating this world. Getting in touch with the mythic quality of life through literature and drama can help us to see the patterns we create in our own lives, particularly how our inner explanations of the way things are partially determine the outer events that happen to us.

Cassie, an ex-nun, provides an example of how this works. When I first met with her she did little but weep. The sessions contained long, blank pauses which seemed to accurately reflect the life she was leading. Living alone and working at a bookkeeping job that in no way reflected her intellectual ability or academic achievements, she took no initiative in establishing a social life and turned aside any attempts by others to get to know her. She described herself in the past as a victim of circumstances and the bad will of others. However, my perception of her strengths grew, particularly as she made good use of symbolism in fantasies. Her inward journey is more fully described later but here I wish to note how large amounts of related reading, much of it fiction, and one film facilitated her treatment.

She was not in touch with her own actions which maneuvered others into doing the *wrong thing* which she then judged as their fault and used to justify her victim role and immobility. I suggested she read Laurens van der Post's *Venture to the Interior,* a tale of an African safari that can also be read as a journey to the interior of the psyche, and two of Joseph Conrad's novels, *Heart of Darkness* and the *Secret Sharer.* She became more aware of her suppression of the dark side of her character, the anger and bad will which she had not owned and experienced as coming from others. She was much like the white men the books dealt with, who denied and feared their own instinctual nature. They scapegoated and projected their aggression and sexuality onto the natives. We used other books, Sheila Moon's *Knee Deep in Thunder,* a fantasy that describes a journey with some very strange characters and how they all are needed to manage various obstacles along the way. She came to identify various sub-personalities in herself, some of which she did not like, who nevertheless had an importance in managing her life. She went to the movie "Walkabout" (a story of an Australian aborigine who rescues and travels with a young woman and her brother; finally, not being really understood or seen, he dies). She recognized her situation in these art forms, saw that she had the option of responding and saying *yes* to newly discovered instinctual elements within her or *no* and letting them die. She did not let them die. She astonished me in a group session a couple of months later by casually remarking to one of the men, "You really turn me on." He did. They have been comfortably married for a couple of years now.

Art therapy is a life-quickening process. It is not meant to substitute for the relationships of the real world, but it provides means for comprehending them and for trying new behavior. The feeling of being fully alive and confident of their own ability to continue growth is at a peak when clients end the intensive phase of treatment. This tapers off in the months that follow, but in my follow-up one to two years later they generally report feeling more integrated than before and they know more about the stimuli to old patterns which they either avoid or use differently. There are lapses but also periods of remembering to remember that tide them over. More importantly, they have made decisions and tried out different behavior and they are being seen and related to by the people who matter to them in ways which confirm the direction they are going.

This book utilizes my experience as a psychotherapist, it is a guide for people undertaking this pilgrimage to knowing themselves. I will accompany you for a portion of the way, describing the journey inward with art experiences which will uncover (or discover) the ways in which you limit yourself, will show you the autonomy and choice you possess, and ways of awakening images from the inner depths to guide you in choosing direction. Then we will discuss the creative process as the central part of the inward journey in light of the three major systems of theory: Transactional Analysis, Gestalt Experience, and Jungian Depth Psychology.

Right now I am not in touch with the growing places or love from other people. I feel trapped in a well but I know I am not only the trapped part but that which can call out. I keep myself trapped by not calling out.

THE INWARD JOURNEY

I

You are about to begin creating images that can guide you into your deeper self. In the course of your journey, art experiments are suggested which can evoke associations and insights into the wider dimensions within, underneath your conscious self. You must supply a space to work in, either a quiet room or a comfortable natural setting, and the materials. You can work alone or in a group.

A word about materials. Different aspects of you, like different personalities, need different art media to express what wants to be said. Since you will be acting out with materials and words the most neglected parts of yourself, you may need to experiment with a range of materials to find what feels right to express these feelings.

Some possibilities:

CLAY   Slippery, gritty, oozy between your fingers, hardening, lumpy, good to pound, to carve when it is soft, to scratch when it is hard, to throw, fling, roll, pinch, shape, and create something that never existed before.

PAINT   Large jars of poster paint that you can use to drip, dribble, and splash, maybe having run water over the drawing sheet beforehand to let the colors merge and blend and swirl out as you shake the page; explore brush possibilities (or sponge or twigs or your own fingers and hands) making all kinds of lines, wiggly, thin, wide, nervous, firm, strong, teasing with short strokes or long, looping, free, funny. You don't have to please anybody or make anything pretty, or neat, or significant.

CRAYONS AND OTHER COLOR   Craypas are half crayons and half pastels—take the paper off so you can use the side for broad strokes, felt-tip pens, charcoal sticks, india ink—all have their own particular language possibilities. Wax crayons, rubbed hard on paper, resist colored inks painted over them and become brilliant, jewel-like lines or blotches.

Things can be combined. After paint has dried, a twig dipped into black india ink creates exciting line possibilities—try some with your awkward hand, the one you usually do not use in writing; it is freer to do things differently, not perfectly.

PAPERS AND COLLAGE MATERIALS   Collage materials can be added with glue to papers of all kinds, newspapers, grocery sacks, slick surfaces, absorbent tissues. Collage materials can be almost anything but it is easy to start with portions of pictures cut from magazines, whatever catches your eye. Include old photographs of you, combine them to make something absurd, or to make a statement through connections that really interest you.

PLAY and DISCOVER!

In order to guide yourself, you must know where you are before you begin the journey. And since you will be both the explorer and the explored, you had best check your present position and orient yourself clearly before you move from the familiar you into areas that may seem strange and foreign. So, to find out where you are now we will take the first step.

THE SELF BOX

Materials you will need: a cardboard box, scissors, glue, and a pile of old picture magazines. You are going to make a three-dimensional representation of you. It does not have to be a box, any shape with an inside and an outside will do.

Make something that feels right to you in terms of size, depth, breadth. Starting with a cardboard box, you can cut the openings that allow other people to see inside. Determine what you keep on the inside of you. What do you choose to show on the outside? Represent these. Paint if you choose or glue on parts of magazine pictures, materials, and favorite objects.

When you have finished, think about what you have placed in the center, what you have included that you prefer to keep hidden, what you have not included. If you are making this along with a group that will talk together after, you may be startled to realize you left out some major aspect of the way other people see you. Did you include anything from your past, any hopes or fears, what you feel bad about yourself, what you like about yourself? Add them now, if you wish.

How did you go about the process of constructing your image? Did you do it quickly, knowing with sureness the way it should be? Perhaps a bit carelessly, thinking more of the idea you wanted to represent rather than whether the construction would stand? Or did you feel your way slowly?

In making the Self Box you experienced yourself in an active, unique and unrepeatable way. You formed a visible, graphic record of your perception of you; you integrated your reality with fantasy through the art materials.

Oddly enough, everything you did shouted what you are. This construction is as uniquely you as your thumbprint or your handwriting. Your style in both the material you selected and the way you went about your construction, your process, can be seen as the essence of you shining through every choice.

"But I'm not an artist," you may protest, "if I were, this would look better." Skill with the use of art materials is not the point. You played with material and created possibilities with what you found. You are not concerned here with ART but with using materials to extend your awareness of your own experience possibilities. You want to rediscover the naive wisdom you had as a child. Of course you are not Picasso. You are you. You are finding out more about you and not comparing or ranking with anyone. You are *unique.*

Jennie, who most often thought of herself as a wife and mother, constructed a box made of mirrors on the outside. It was difficult to find the opening, but once inside the mirrors completely fell away and the box revealed pictures of deep sea creatures of intense color and beauty as well as pictures of dark painful wounds. As she talked of her box it became clear that she had spent her life reflecting what she thought the people around her wanted to see. She kept the dark side of life, her hurts and anger, hidden even from herself much of the time. The cost was high. Her vivid inner beauty was not visible either.

Ben, on the other hand, had a construction which seemed carelessly put together at first glance, yet on closer inspection, it held a wealth of detail. Images of masculine competitiveness vied for room with delicate flower-like women and sensuous fantasies. He had placed a small box within the larger one and this opened to a mathematically precise construction of wooden toothpicks. He was at a loss to account for this but somehow he knew it was important. There was something more in him to be discovered which he did not yet understand.

Two examples of self boxes: The top one covered with foil opens up to a world of color and organic forms. The lower box is meant to hang; it has passageways filled with a candle, feathers, wheat stalks, etc. A sea shell in the center is suspended in a net. Each represents how the maker felt about his inner life.

Your box may not be as elaborate as these but when it is finished, it too can tell you more than you knew you intended. Look at it carefully and notice the questions it raises. These are small signals of what needs to be explored and of what needs to be transformed on the journey you are beginning.

YOUR LIFETIME

Materials you will need: A large piece of paper at least 24" x 36", poster paints, felt-tip pens, or charcoal.

Imagine that this paper represents the whole of your lifetime, the beginning, the now, the future and the end. First sit quietly for a few minutes, then fill it however you choose. Don't expect anything, or try, or analyze, just allow your mind to be quiet, to let happen what will by simply holding the thought: *This is my lifetime.*

When you have finished be aware of the quality of your breathing and how your body feels, and how it felt to be totally absorbed with the making. Where do you feel the most excitement? What did you discover? What do you want to share?

Ann started clockwise from the lower part of her sheet with dull monochromatic colors for the portion which represented her childhood, gradually brightening them as she proceeded into young womanhood after the sad, dark, heavy lines representing her experience of high school, blazing out with joyful colors with the birth of her first child, shifting into clear blues and greens as she represented the struggle to define herself as a person loving and related to her family but separate from them. Three quarters around she left the future blank.

Molly approached the project from a completely different angle. In the top left corner of her sheet was a multicolored ball which gradually appeared to unravel across the page developing various angles and color possibilities. The whole sheet was covered with paint. "I haven't finished," she explained "but this is what I intend, to experience every possibility I can imagine."

Kate's picture looked more like a conventional landscape yet the symbols held specific meaning for her. A road, her life, stretched from the bottom left hand side of the page and seemed to disappear in the middle, a place of centering where a sun, conscious awareness, was rising. She placed a crescent moon, which to her represented the phases of her womanhood, over the sun. On the left, a tree with its forking roots visible stood by a stream, representing her inner experience with herself, and a mountain with a house on the right represented her relationship with others.

The three pictures, very different from one another, emerged as each woman faced the blankness of the sheet and allowed herself to feel what was the meaning of her lifetime and how to depict it. Each discovered a central theme or pattern. Two stressed how they *felt* about their lives; one, how she *thought* about it. Look at your lifetime painting. Does it show more about the way you think or about the way you feel about your life? Does it have a center or is it linear like an ongoing story? What are the themes and questions in it?

If you answer these questions with certainty, you are ready to move to the beginnings, how it all began, how you came to be you.

Where your journey began and what baggage you have carried from that time.

When you were a child you got a lot of messages and instructions about how to be you from your family. You not only learned manners, how to dress, what friends to choose and such, but also you picked up some of your parents' attitudes towards life, particularly their view of your worth and your importance or lack of it. One way of exploring what these messages were is by sculpting what your family felt like when you were growing up.

What we are investigating in this chapter is how YOU came to think about yourself in the ways you do and perhaps limit yourself in the ways you do. You want to clear away distortions picked up from how other people have viewed you and how you have responded in order to reach the sense of you now deciding your own fate, setting your own goals.

THE FAMILY SCULPTURE

Materials you will need: a good double handful of clay, paper, and pencil.

First, close your eyes and go back to a time in your childhood, somewhere between two and eight years old. Think about the members in your family. Who was around? How old were they? How did you feel about them?

Note on the paper two or three adjectives describing each person. Take the clay and make a sculpture of the adjectives describing one particular person, e.g., if you described Dad as *warm but critical*, you might make just an arm reaching out

---

from a ball with a lot of sharp points. The idea is not to make a figure of a person, but something that gives a feeling of how that person felt to you when you were younger.

When you have sculpted each family member in turn, put them in relation to each other to show who felt close and who was far away from you emotionally. You might show who was on top and who was under someone else in the family.

You now have a sculpture that shows what it felt like to be growing up in the family into which you were born. Look at it carefully and sense what your sculpture might indicate that you had not thought of before. Write one question or comment from each family member in the sculpture to you, and then your comment or question to each family member.

The Family of Your Past

The way you discover how you got to be the way you are is to look at the messages from the family of your birth and the decisions you made about them. The messages you wrote from the sculpture are some of the instructions you received about what you should do and what to avoid to gain approval. You may have been told how to be a winner; you may have been told how to be a loser. Some of the problematic messages had to do with *not* being you: "Be perfect"; "Don't be silly"; "Don't be a child."

As a child you learned to behave in ways that got you some attention. Even if it was not the kind you wanted most, it was better than none. Certain feelings or actions were associated with that attention: getting on the honor roll or playing dumb, throwing a tantrum, being awkward and spilling

things, becoming a rebel, or being a victim to get comfort and feel justified—any one of these could have become a favorite role for manipulating the attention you needed.

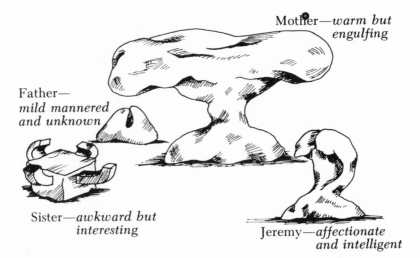

Mother—*warm but engulfing*

Father—*mild mannered and unknown*

Sister—*awkward but interesting*

Jeremy—*affectionate and intelligent*

So much more comes out in the sculpture than can be said in words. Jeremy, a bright young lawyer, in doing his family sculpture pictured his mother *warm but engulfing* as a large mushroom in the center of the family circle, his father *mild mannered and unknown* a small lumpish object hidden from his view by the mother figure, and his sister *awkward but interesting* a squarish object with a large number of arm-like protuberances. He depicted himself as an ocean wave, a slightly less bulky figure than his mother but tending towards her form.

The central importance of his mother was clear, as was the absence of a direct relationship with his father and the similar structure of his own identity to that of his mother. Her messages to him were: "Don't be you. Be important as I would like to be." Jeremy had bought her program: he was active in school politics, president of his student body, head of his class in law school. Only now at 35 was he waking up to realize that he hated all forms of competition and that the profession for which he had prepared himself held no interest for him.

A good clue in understanding your own functioning is to think about the feeling with which you are most familiar

now—competitive, jealous, angry, depressed, dumb. It just might be that you are collecting feelings of a particular kind. A feeling prompts you to use your energy to get your needs met, then the feeling goes away. If you have a particular feeling much of the time or in many situations, then chances are that you are not using it to identify what you want changed and doing something about it. Instead you are expecting someone else to do something and you are collecting that old familiar feeling that you used to associate with some kind of attention in your family. If showing hurt feelings in your family did not pay because they were ignored, you may have learned to attack with a temper tantrum which got some action. Today you might find when you are ready to explode with anger, you are actually hiding a feeling of hurt inside. The attention you got then and get now will never satisfy the hurt because it is not acknowledged. In Transactional Analysis

this is known as a *Racket.* That is a rough word to use, but when you know that almost everybody has a favorite bad feeling he/she tends to collect, there is a bracing quality, almost like a cold shower, in calling your particular bad feeling a racket. This is especially true if it is something like feeling very unappreciated and sorry for yourself, or smoldering anger. It very quickly changes your accustomed way of looking at things. For example, you can begin to think about what kind of payoff you get from collecting such an ostensibly unhappy feeling. Do you cash it in for something else?

Jeremy discovered he was playing a blaming game of "If it weren't for you..." and "Now see what you've made me do." Staying immobilized and *confused* used to demonstrate to his mother that her ideas weren't so great. It did the same to other people who tried to direct or advise him now.

ANNA'S FAMILY SCULPTURE

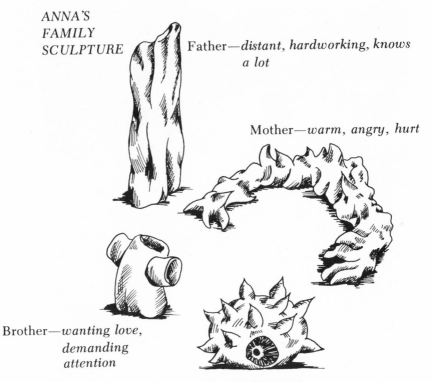

Father—*distant, hardworking, knows a lot*

Mother—*warm, angry, hurt*

Brother—*wanting love, demanding attention*

Anna—*bright, lonely, artistic*

Messages:

from father: "I don't want you. Work hard but you won't be successful."

from mother: "Be what I wanted to be (a dancer) but don't be sexy."

from brother: "Pay attention to me."

from Anna to parents: "I'll work hard at being what you want but I won't succeed and I won't be sexy."

to brother: "I'll pay attention to you rather than me."

When Anna depicted her family she realized she had received messages from her father that life was a struggle; she should work hard but since she was only a girl, she would not count for much. From her mother, Anna heard "Don't be sexy," but also that she should be someone special, probably a professional dancer as her mother had wanted to be. For a long time Anna took lessons, practiced and struggled to become a dancer. It did not occur to her that she had combined and was acting out her parents' directions—a struggling, nonsexy dancer was certainly not going to count for much!

A Racket feeling always covers up another feeling that could be used to change the situation, but for some reason that feeling was really scary to feel as a child, so the child used and started collecting this substitute feeling instead. In Anna's family, anger was quite unacceptable. Being sad on the other hand was O.K. and she could get a backrub or some attention. So gradually whenever there was stress or trouble and some anger would be called up in Anna, she learned to suppress it and feel sad instead. As time went on this felt quite natural, almost like that was how one should feel, e.g., helpless and sad when a bully took a toy instead of angry and capable of getting it back. As a result, Anna lost much of her power to take care of herself, which closely fitted her father's idea of what a woman was and confirmed his message that she *wouldn't count for much.*

Let's look again at your own family sculpture. Look at it for the feelings it sets up in you, then go over the list of messages from family members to determine the instructions which told you how to be, how to get attention, how to manage your life. Now look at your own messages to find out how you did or did not buy the program, the decisions you made about you. Children do not have to buy the destructive messages. But most of them do, a little. Jeremy had bought the "Don't be you, be what I want you to be." He now had to decide to be himself. Fortunately, most children grow up with two parents and often a grandparent or an older brother or sister who give them options in ways of looking at themselves.

Your Here and Now Family

We now have arrived at the second level of analysis—here and now. Look at each message again. Is anyone currently saying the same thing to you? Your boyfriend, girlfriend, boss, husband, wife, an associate? (It is almost incredible how many people find all, or nearly all, of the early messages now being sensed coming from their spouses.) To whom are you currently sending your old messages? If you discover there is a strong carry-over, you are now in a position to clear away some of the major distortions in your relationships. Anna was dismayed to realize she was sending the same messages she had received as a child now to her husband, i.e., "I don't know whether I want you; work hard but you won't be successful; pay attention to me."

The basic idea is that from your early decisions and feelings you probably built up a repertoire of two to five predictable sets of interactions with other people which you use to get the attention you feel you need. The setups you may be using to collect the familiar feelings can be infuriating to other people or fascinating and sometimes even amusing but they always serve to structure time and your energy in ways that prevent much real closeness to anyone and stifle growth.

It is important to understand the family messages or injunctions about how to be and your childhood decisions, in order to learn that you can make a new decision. This means a redecision on some of those crucial early injunctions you originally accepted. Anna, in the here and now of looking at her family sculpture, thought about where she was now hearing messages similar to those early ones. Although she had a tendency to think her husband did not value her sexually, she basically knew this message was coming from herself alone and she had never taken the risk of trying to be definitely attractive. She did not want to make mistakes which she thought would bring ridicule. When she probed this sore place she remembered feeling humiliated when she thought her father had laughed at her as a little girl in her first bathing suit. She now saw that keeping this memory was perhaps part of her early decision to collect sadness and follow mother's message not to be sexy. She realized that she never visited the boutique stores whose clothes intrigued her but instead shopped sales for sensible clothes. She looked at her well-tailored but drab dress of brown checks and added, "I hate this outfit. I feel like a stick in it. It's about time I made a redecision. I don't have to keep telling myself to buy clothes that will last and avoid the things that would be fun for only a single season."

Anna had moved to another level of looking at the family sculpture as a picture of herself, a depiction of aspects of the early family that she had hidden inside. In the language of psychology these are *introjects*. The introjected messages sound like they are coming from you. (When you hear the family messages coming from others, it is known as *projection*.) Introjected parent messages have a lot of *shoulds* and *oughts*. They are often phrased in the second person as you talk to yourself inside. Often they are variants, of course, of the messages you wrote from family members in your sculpture.

Anna, when she thought of the sculpture as a picture of herself, had to question what in her was like her strong masculine father? She determined this was her nursing role which she had developed after giving up the idea of a dancing career. She decided that a change was necessary in the sculpture as a picture of herself; the hurt feminine aspect of her needed to be cared for and helped to risk growing and the bright and curious child aspect in her needed more room to explore. She moved the clay figures closer.

"I choose to be me, not mother's idea of me, and that means connecting more with my body (here she placed the

sculpture of herself, a head with spikey bumps, on top of the headless body of her infant brother sculpture). I love to dance though not professionally. I love to make things and use my hands. I haven't done this for years, but I choose to *now*. The strong masculine and the wounded feminine aspects in me make a good pair when they are related (here she placed the masculine tower within the crescent of the feminine). I block myself when I keep them apart."

Anna's work illustrates the meditative possibilities in working. As she looked at the problematic aspects of her family sculpture she began to sense the strengths and where certain feeling energy in the family had been misdirected. This raised questions, e.g., if her parents could have been more caring to one another, then could the parts of her which were like those parents, her masculine power and feminine vulnerability be brought closer? Her potential for becoming an integrated whole person became clearer. You might write a similar outline for your own sculpture.

Redecisions and Revisions

As some of the above works for you, come back to the sculpture again, looking at it now in terms of your goal of reaching a more creative, inclusive sense of self. You can't reject, deny, or throw out any part of what you have been, but you can work with it and come to a different relationship particularly with those parts you do not like and want to repress. You can find out what strengths there might be, what odd, perverse blessings these unchosen, unwanted aspects and experiences can hold for you. Often, just playing with the figures, putting them into different combinations, relating mother to father in a different way, can suggest possibilities about the interplay of your own strengths and weaknesses. Writing these insights, sharing them with another or others helps to strengthen the redecision. It also gives the *inner self* some elements to play with. Once we have acknowledged an image and seriously worked with it, even when we lay the work aside, further ramifications continue to suggest themselves, occasionally in thought and often in dreams.

THE LANGUAGE OF DREAMS

An alternative view of what is happening now

Your inner self uses a language quite different from the grammar of verbs and nouns in sentences. Initially, the signals you become aware of are the images in your dreams. To decode the language, start to reflect on these images, recall your dreams.

The best approach to analysis of a dream is to view it in the same way you look at a painting, listen to a song, or read a poem. Probably it is saying something meaningful with the most economical use of vivid, concentrated images possible. Consider those images, particularly the ones that recur frequently. They distill often paradoxical facts and emotions into a single statement. They are the elements of a language that comes straight from *your* depths.

It is not quite accurate to say they are the voice of the inner self, but they are closely related, and learning to read them is an important step in getting to know that unknown self.

Working with images from dreams as they emerge from the unconscious, relating to them, connecting them to the events and relationships in your conscious life causes you to sense an emerging pattern. Dreams disconnect some things and connect others in ways you would not consciously consider. If you pay close attention to your dreams, it begins to seem as if you are in a kind of dialogue with another. The dream is like a poem letter you receive which makes some comments on your concerns. Suddenly, it appears that certain figures seem to be recurring more frequently and acting in different ways in your dreams.

PAINTING AND TALKING WITH YOUR DREAM

It is useful to paint or draw the images of the dream to begin to get a sense of the underlying pattern which is emerging. Painting allows more of you to be involved than just your mind, but it also involves conscious choices in depicting and gives you (the conscious ego part of you) time to reflect on the image. Now you can give it a voice and *listen*. First, describe yourself as the image, e.g., "I'm an elevator in a tall building; I take people to the heights and the depths of the building down far into the subbasement. There's not much room in me; I can only take a few people at a time. My movement is always vertical; I have little to do with the horizontal. I run on only one track though, and I feel quite empty when I am not in use." Then you respond and the image answers. You are writing a dialogue.

Sometimes, describing yourself as the image is enough. The meaning, the analogy connecting the image to your everyday life, flashes through you; the linking can be dramatic, often bringing tears. The elevator image above was from one of my dreams when too much of my life was being lived in my work role as a psychotherapist. The same image, however, can have different meanings for different people. As in a poem, the meaning has to be established within the context of the whole dream and the allusions of the individual dreamer.

Each person has some few symbols with highly idiosyncratic meanings that recur almost like a signature, giving an originality in style and emotion to a dream series. A young, hippie girl at Esalen, with whom Fritz Perls once

worked,voiced the same image: "I'm an elevator. I get used all the time. Men come into me and go out again..." Her surface pose as a sexually liberated woman covered a sense of being used, abandoned, and hurt. The dream brought this aspect to her attention and posed the question whether she chose to continue this or to risk acknowledging her need for great autonomy and making the change in lifestyle that would allow it.

Decoding the Dream

The Gestalt method of decoding dreams works mostly with the unconscious personal aspects of your situation or the functions that you do not consciously think of as your own. Using this method, you view everything that occurs in the dream as a part of yourself. When you have an unresolved conflict, the unconscious works at resolving it through dreaming. Each object in the dream, as well as each person and the setting itself, is an aspect of you that the dream is connecting in a different way than your conscious mind usually thinks.

To understand this suggested new wholeness, play the role, give a voice to each object or person in the dream. Look at your painting to decide the two images that are most unlike each other and create dialogue like writing a play, give a voice to each image *character* in turn. Getting them to come to an *understanding* can bring the deep issues of the dream to your conscious awareness.

Anna, whose family sculpture we looked at in the last chapter, had the following dream: "I am attending a conference in Hawaii. Something I have said has been misunderstood. Someone says I have many friends here, but I see Susan (a rival) and think to myself that I don't trust anyone here and I will stick to myself. A woman indicates she would like me to join the group for dinner at Pearl Harbor, a place not many tourists think to go. While at dinner, I notice a woman dressed in black and white whose hat is like a set of matches, eating at a table below ours. Later, I am removing leaves from an herb garden that has been neglected. They have lost all flavor and I throw them out."

She drew the dream and went on to write the following dialogue:

Anna to Pearl Harbor Restaurant: You're a very odd place to take nourishment, a symbol of infamy and sneak attacks.
Restaurant: You have come here and now I offer food.
Anna: Food for angry thoughts of past grievances.

Anna to Woman: Your hat is unusual and quite dangerous, it seems to me.
Woman (laughs): You think I might turn into a *hothead*, but I disguised this as a remarkable and elegant head cover.
Anna: A hat is for protection, but that is no protection for your head.
Woman: Don't be absurd. In the dark ages, hats were for protection, this is something else. I'm quite carefully dressed in black and white convictions and if I give the impression that my head is easily ignited, so much the better—elegant passion.
Anna: You seem to be mocking me using these things for show. I have deep convictions but I don't trivialize them and make a dangerous spectacle of myself.
Woman: We each have our self-righteous trip.

In the process of dialogue, Anna began to connect the current unacknowledged anger she was feeling toward her husband (under her Racket feeling of hurt at being misunderstood). She began to realize how she was taking nourishment for these feelings not from her present situation so much as from a place of past grievances where the issues of betrayal had once seemed very black and white. The volatile headgear was a vivid symbol of current anger which she had not previously identified.

Relating the Painting to the Dream

In your painting of the dream, you selected the important elements and related them to one another in placement on the paper. What did this add to your understanding? Do the kinds of images on the right differ from the left? The top from the bottom? Is there something in the center of your painting or is it empty? What do these positions mean to you? Is there any one object more dominant than the others? What would it do to the painting to shrink the dominant image and give a less conspicuous object more prominence?

In Anna's painting, she placed the hat of matches in the center which emphasized the central importance of the easily ignited or endangered head (thought processes). The herbs without flavor on the left side she thought of as past grievances which, she ruefully admitted, used to flavor her life but now had lost their flavor and she was ready to throw them out.

The object of this further play is simply that the conversation goes on. Tonight is another night and further dreams come. When you begin to work with your dreams this way, the character of your dreams changes and assumes a more purposeful direction. You notice more recurring symbols. A particular vocabulary of characters and symbols is building which begins to tap down into a source of meanings beneath the personal level of your life. Your dialogue with your dreams holds the possibility of gradually bringing you into relationship with the content deep inside your being and to symbols which foreshadow the wholeness towards which you are working. Relating to the images, connecting them to the events and relationships in your conscious life, causes a shifting of patterns. Anna's working with her dream of Pearl Harbor enabled her to see how past betrayals in her own life could inflame her current situation. Her next dreams continued with a restaurant theme but a different kind of *nourishment.*

Painting of a dream: *A bull and two cows are struggling to catch up with the family to which they belong. They are exhausted. A wise woman appears and makes cheese from their milk. She offers it to me but I am repulsed because of its vile smell. A girl like myself appears and tells me this is a very special food which I should accept.*

The painting emphasizes the primitive force and power of the instincts which can be transformed into a food to nourish the feminine development if she can overcome her repugnance and disgust. Elements in us which we consciously reject, hold a potential for our growth, a theme found frequently in fairy tales as well as dreams.

The total dream, coming as it does at a particular point in the dreamer's life, offers a comment on the present and frequently points a direction of development in the future. Lynn, a 25-year-old publishing house editor, had the following dream after the third session of her intensive treatment week:

Painting of a dream: *I have entered into a flirtation with a man. We are in a boat at sea and he drowns. I am helpless to rescue him.*

This dream frightened the dreamer and raised questions about her unconsciousness and irresponsibility in a current relationship, an alternative view and strong contrast to her conscious viewpoint.

I am beginning a trip to India. I join a family who are on a journey around the world. When we arrive in India, I am supposed to camp in a site this side of the Ganges River which my mother has described as beautiful and restful but when we arrive we find it is smelly, dangerous, and filled with thieves so we decide to go on. We are about to cross the Ganges River and I expect to encounter an unpleasant man described by my mother when she visited India years ago with my father. He guards the ferry and exploits his passengers. To my surprise I find the river is no more than a yard or so across for we are quite near the source. The man at the crossing simply questions me: do I want to cross? and I say yes, for my goal is a city on

the other side, he guides me over. My mother seems to
have joined us at this point and in bafflement says:
"Things are not as they were."

Lynn was nonplussed by her dream. She had no religious
interests and was turned off by both the Jesus-freaking of her
younger sister and by the Eastern-style meditation/mysticism
of her roommate. Yet this dream she felt had some sort of
religious significance.

She said: "India is a very foreign place to me, a place of
the rich and the very poor. It has produced many wise men
and it is a place where wisdom is sought. I dream of it now because I seem to have begun a journey to foreign, unknown
parts of myself. I am finding new feelings and conflicting
thoughts within me. Yesterday and the day before when we
worked on my relationship to my parents, I found out things I
don't know what to do with, even how to think about them."

I suggested we look at the dreams with this in mind. She
was on a journey but she was not alone, a family was there.
She viewed them as healthy, happy, and adventurous; they
were both a model of wholeness and a resource to her. The
first encampment, the one urged on her by her mother, she
rejected because she saw that it was not the place that her
mother had imagined. This part of the dream Lynn connected
to her view of her mother's role in life, a role of letting herself
be exploited. The dream picture of a dangerous camp of
thieves was an exaggeration of the awareness which had been
growing in Lynn that early in her life her mother had placed
herself in a position where her own development would be cut
off and she had then rationalized her choice. She seemed to be
self sufficient, invulnerable, and strong, a woman looked up to
in her community and highly valued, yet her daughter knew
her to be totally cut off from any real feelings of relatedness.
She had no anger, no passion, no depth—she had been robbed
of these and she denied her awareness. Lynn had been
following her mother's footsteps.

Lynn went on with her exploration of the dream. The sacred river Ganges, the place of cleansing, had to be forded. For months prior to treatment, Lynn had been shaken by spells of unaccountable tears. They seemed fed by a river within her that would never end. Now she was close to the source. *Her* vision had been cleansed. She could see her goal, the sacred city in the distance. She could see the river was fordable and she simply had to ask to find the help she needed in crossing. She did not yet know who this masculine ferry keeper was within her but she knew she could count on his assistance. When she did, her mother would join her and things "would not be as they were."

This was a profoundly moving dream to both of us because it so clearly confirmed the work she had begun and the direction in which she would go.

Apart from the dialogues and written work with dreams, some art exercises can be used to deepen your experience of these aspects within. The art exercises which follow are designed to help you identify and contact two major inner realities: aspects of your sex that are most difficult for you to admit you own, and qualities of the opposite sex which you possess—the inner man in every woman, the inner woman in every man.

First, create a picture of how these parts relate to each other and to your goal of bringing to consciousness your creative inner self. In growing up, you probably disowned certain parts of your personality because they did not seem to fit with what other people expected of you and you enlarged those qualities that received approval, e.g., in America, we generally value personal openness, sociability, and material achievement so these qualities probably were reinforced in you as a child and gradually your contrary qualities, which weren't valued highly, were disguised and repressed. A lot of imagination and creative ability associated with the contrary qualities may have dried up in you as you became less

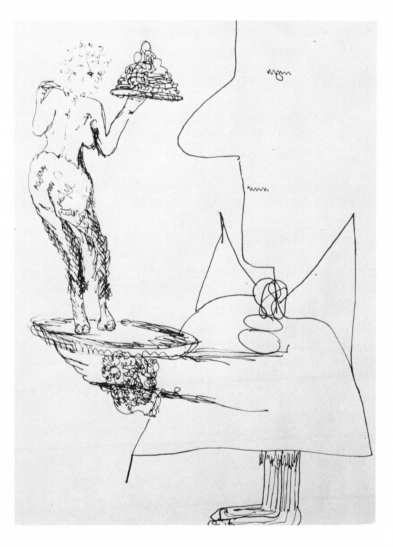

A Gestalt Doodle: *I began with no idea of what might develop, drew a line which turned into a man, then a tray appeared on which he was serving up a female satyr. She in turn developed a tray and is ready to serve someone else. It doesn't need a title; it's just fun to let go and see what comes.*

spontaneous. All of these disowned emotional components are called the *shadow* or *dark self.*

In addition, there is another unfamiliar part which might be called the inner woman in every man and the inner man in every woman. In a way that was similar to the development of your shadow side, you very likely repressed aspects of you and your experiences that did not correspond to the attributes your own sex is supposed to possess, e.g., a boy should be self-confident, assertive, logical. Qualities he regards as feminine, like tears, get pushed down, and the same thing happens with girls repressing their masculine intelligence or boisterousness or interest in mechanics.

As you begin to look for your inner self these parts push to be recognized. They appear in symbolic form in dreams (Anna's hotheaded woman was a shadow figure) but we can also consciously contact them through art as the following experiments suggest.

It seems when I get depressed, I am beating myself without mercy.

MEETING YOUR DARK SELF

Material you will need: a heap of old magazines, *Life* and *Look* used to be the richest source of supply for images, but any magazine that has pictures of human feelings and conditions will do. Scissors, gluestick, a pencil, scratch paper, and sturdy background paper.

First, note on the scratch paper all the characteristics of persons of *your own sex* who really get to you in a negative way, e.g., as a woman you may not be able to stand other women who are bitchy, controlling, whiney, manipulative, whatever, but specify the qualities that for you are the most obnoxious.

Go through the magazines and cut or tear out images that represent these qualities. When you have collected a sufficient pile, sift through and find those that really hold the essence for you and start your collage by gluing these in the center of your background sheet. Continue with the others.

When you have finished, spend some time looking at your production. You might pin it on your wall and live with it for a week before doing the next step, a dialogue. When you are ready, do a written exercise giving the collage a voice and writing the dialogue as it flows. It will flow as soon as you begin to consider this as an inner aspect which you have not given sufficient attention.

This experience can be illuminating. In one group, a minister's wife, middle-aged and beautiful but mild-looking, produced an hysterically funny collage which gave great prominence to a football helmeted and togged blond young woman, plus several images of Raquel Welch as a tough, mud-spattered, sexy roller derby winner. The following week, she tried to relate to this aspect within her and allowed it some room to act. She reported an astonishing success in a difference of opinion with her usually dictatorial husband. Another woman in the same group, but far more earthy, used a picture of a blond socialite whom she described as a phoney, ladylike manipulator. After acting *her* for a week, she had so many interesting reactions from her children, the plumber and the grocery clerk, she decided maybe there was some aspects of this symbol she could use validly after all.

CONTACTING THE INNER MAN IN EVERY WOMAN/THE INNER WOMAN IN EVERY MAN

The art exercise to relate to the inner elements of the opposite sex within you is the same as with the dark self, only here you select pictures related to both the very positive and the very negative feeling responses you have toward the opposite sex. *Playboy* and *Sports Illustrated* have many pictures involving plastic, sexual sterotypes, but also try to find pictures which capture your individual feelings.

Getting in touch with these inner opposites gives not only an uncomfortable sense of recognition of some of these patterns as they exist in you, but it may help you to view others whom you have despised in a more objective way. Owning and recognizing your own qualities gives you a fuller sense of who you are and releases energy that was tied up in keeping your self-image *clean.*

The guide in choosing a different direction

Once you begin to listen to the alternative points of view that your inner self suggests to you, you will find that you can carry on a dialogue with it about your life situations, problems, and possibilities. There are a number of processes that facilitate this conversation using your body, music, and art materials. You will find media provide different levels of experience.

Meditation, Painting, Music, and Mandalas

The many forms of meditation all propose to awaken a deeper consciousness. Most emphasize specific body positions, others involve movement. All involve stopping your ordinary activity and thought to allow an opportunity for different types of perception to emerge. Robert Ornstein, who has done research on the psychology of consciousness and meditation, uses an analogy, "You have to turn off the sun in order to see the stars." If you are not familiar with meditation, Shunryo Suzuki's *Zen Mind, Beginner's Mind* or Alan Watts' *The Essence of Alan Watts - Meditation* provides a start, but do not feel restricted to the presently popular Eastern techniques.

Basically, the first step is to release the body from its normal tensions. The easiest way to do this is to concentrate on your breathing. You can either sit comfortably erect or lie on the floor, flat on your back. Stay focused on your breath rhythm and count your exhalations. As thoughts come in, let them pass without getting involved with them. Let your attention be on your breathing. As you breathe out, envision the tensions of your body, the obstructions and static of your thoughts, draining away leaving an emptiness and receptivity. Hold the exhalation for a few seconds before taking a breath, then envision taking in, opening up to the energy and nourishment from without that you need. After awhile, the mental static which fills your mind during the day will clear away and you will be in a meditative state. Five minutes each day followed by a period of work with art will produce interesting progress in your use of art material.

MEETING THE INNER OTHER IN PAINT

Material you will need: a large sheet of drawing paper and a set of colors—poster paints, water colors, felt-tip pens. Select a color that appeals to you without thought of what you are going to paint. Make a single mark on the paper of whatever size or shape seems right. Stop. Look at the colored portion and alternately at the shape of the non-colored portion. Allow yourself to sense what the next shape and color should be in relation to what is there. Proceed stopping each time between complete strokes to *look* and *listen.*

These paintings should be dated and collected without looking at them again for a period of several weeks. The development and progress in your choices and use of color shapes and symbols will be more apparent after you have several to refer to.

Louisa Jenkins, a renowned mosaicist whose art processes always include meditation, showed me a freeing-the-body painting exercise she uses to begin work. She spread newspapers on the floor of her studio and after performing relaxation exercises took two thick brushes, one in each hand, dipped them in a black india ink mixture, and standing over the paper bending from the waist, she began with both arms making large strokes much like calligraphy.

Music, carefully chosen, facilitates preparation. Louis Savary in *Passages: A Guide for Pilgrims of the Mind* writes of trance induction exercises for achieving altered states of consciousness. The basic reasons for wanting access to an altered state is to allow the perceptions and connections to emerge which are not available in ordinary everyday consciousness. In Savary's most recent book, *Music and Your*

Mind: Listening with a New Consciousness, he opens a further dimension, working with the multitude of mood and feeling potentialities in music. In my therapy groups and some workshops, I use cassette tapes he and Helen Bonney have developed which are available to the public from the Maryland Institute for Music and Consciousness. A typical selection of music is described in the suggested experience below.

Savary visualizes consciousness as a many-storied skyscraper. Its ground floor represents ordinary consciousness, the state of mind we use normally in thinking, feeling, problem-solving, remembering, and so on. But there are many higher and deeper levels of consciousness, whole floors devoted to

creativity in art, music, invention, mathematics, deep memory, the collective unconscious and dreams, transpersonal, mystical and religious experiences. The building has an elevator and there are old and new techniques in addition to drugs, that can get you off the ground floor to bring you to the other levels. The techniques include biofeedback, sensory deprivation, mind-control, Zen and Transcendental Meditation, and self-hypnosis. Most people, however, seldom go beyond the mind's first floor.

It is one thing to know that these levels exist and wish to explore them, it is another to get there, and still another to know what to do when you get there.

This is my loneliness. I'm on the edge of a gaping hole, a deep pit in the middle of a desert.

AN ALTERED STATE OF CONSCIOUSNESS
WITH GUIDED IMAGERY

What you will need: a quiet room, a stereo phonograph and music which has pleasant-feeling possibilities (Ravel, *Daphis and Chloe;* Brahms, *Symphony No. 1 in C (3rd Movement);* Respighi, *The Pines of Rome;* Debussy, *Girl with the Flaxen Hair*), any music at all that you'd like to feel more deeply.

Relaxation. To feel relaxed is to feel weightless, that the body's muscles are in balance, neither pushing nor pulling. If you are familiar with any relaxation techniques—Zen or Transcendental Meditation, childbirth relaxation exercises, behavior modification, mind control or self-hypnosis —and you find that they help you, by all means use them. In this exercise, comfort is essential. Relax in the way that feels best to you.

One method is to become aware of the various parts of your body relaxing in turn, first your toes, then the foot with its arch, instep, ball, heel, ankle —let go of all effort, rest—the legs, the hands, arms, shoulders, the abdomen, chest, throat, facial muscles, and eyes. It helps to use certain key phrases that eventually become deeply associated with the state of relaxation and trigger it the next time you wish to relax with much less effort—*let go* in a quiet tone of voice. Try to maintain an even rhythm in your breathing. Develop a regular pattern for bringing on this quietly balanced state and practice it often. The more complete the relaxation is, the deeper will be the listening state. In first starting out, it may take up to a half hour to reach a deep state of relaxation, but with practice it will be possible in a few minutes.

Concentration. Once the body is relaxed, your mind is ready to concentrate. This involves focusing your mind on an object as simply and as quietly as you would a camera lens—a flower, a burning candle—and become quietly absorbed in it. Do not analyze, describe, or define it, but receive it in such a way that you can see it in every detail even with your eyes closed. Later, your mind will be able to create its own objects. Every time you exercise your mind power, you are preparing for a fuller listening experience. Many teachers recommend sounding a word or syllable. Humming or intoning a single note and holding it sets up a vibration which affects the entire body and helps it to respond.

The Induction. The goal of this beginners' induction is a summer meadow, a place that you remember having enjoyed and would like to enjoy again now listening to some restful music. Begin by visualizing yourself standing at a doorway. You open a door and before you in the soft twilight mist is a winding mountain path. As you start out with each step, count slowly from ten to zero. At each step, suggest to yourself that the mist will soon disappear and you will sense your warm, sunlit meadow. When you reach zero, allow yourself to feel the change with your feet, your skin, your hearing, and let the music lead you into different experiences in this meadow.

When the music has ended, remain quiet for a minute or so, then suggest to yourself that as the music has ended, you are ready to return to normal consciousness, you will count from three to zero. When you reach zero, you will open your eyes and be in your normal state, fully rested and alert and feeling deeply satisfied. You may want to review the insights gained during the session and tell yourself you will be able to recall them easily whenever you wish.

The exercise above is a beginning. Once you enter the suggested deep state of relaxation, you can begin to listen to music in a new way with your total awareness. You will normally never entirely leave ordinary consciousness, you will continue to hear doors slam and street sounds. Yet your everyday awareness will grow less important as the music itself begins to engage you on other levels of consciousness, for example, memories and dreams, insight, self-evaluation, and creativity.

Almost everyone enters these areas of the mind at one time or another, but few live familiarly with them in the same way that composers, poets, and inventors do. Your mind is able to contain many ideas and experiences at the same time. Music seems to acquire colors, shapes, motion, even taste and scent, and to generate greater levels of emotional intensity and depth when you listen in a state of heightened awareness. Melodies, harmonies, and rhythms open up meanings within you, you see more ways to look at a problem, an idea, a person.

You must practice to reach the deeper levels of altered consciousness, but the above exercise will almost invariably induce a light trance which is characterized by being hyperaware of the music. As you develop familiarity with this process, you can program guided fantasy trips. John Stevens has a number of excellent fantasy exercises in his book *Awareness*, a resource book for exercises which increase the awareness of various senses and different levels of experience in relationships with other people.

One which I use quite frequently in workshops is: Imagine you are out for an evening stroll in a town with which you are familiar and feel safe. As you walk, you pass by a street that is unknown to you but seems interesting. You turn and walk down the left side of the street until you come to a deserted store. As you pass the window, an abandoned object in it catches your eye and you draw closer. Look at it closely, let yourself become the object and imagine your history. Now go back to being you and continue your walk. When the exercise is ended, I suggest that the participants paint a picture of the object.

In discussing these paintings, I find they almost always have a symbolic connection with some experience unfinished or left behind in the individual's life. I ask each person to identify with his painting and describe himself as it. Each is free to discuss his painting as much or as little as he chooses. Others present can make a comment but in the first person and present tense also, thereby owning projections rather than interpreting for another. For example, one man described himself as a clock, "I'm wooden, run down and rusty." Another man looking at the same painting added, "I'm a trifle out of date, but my works are in good order and, with a bit of cleaning out and regular attention, I can function quite well." Each man spoke from and referred to his own emotional feeling.

Often in these fantasies, you will discover the presence of opposite or opposing values and interests. One way to deepen your understanding of these polarities is to meditate on them as you construct a mandala to express the interplay between the elements.

The Mandala. A circle motif in its manifold combinations with the square is one of the great symbols of wholeness. It is commonly found in dreams and also throughout the world in the art of every culture; it is universal in nature. The construction of a mandala involves and satisfies a need for order. It is both a process and a product of meditation. In it you can explore the intrinsic relationship between darkness and light, evil and good, or whatever opposites you want to pair. The yin-yang symbol epitomizes this. When one aspect, yang, the light, reaches its greatest strength, the dark power of yin is born within its depths: "...for night begins at midday when yang breaks up and begins to change into yin."

Jung described constructing a mandala as an expression of a self-healing process through which the psyche maintains its sanity and nurtures its own growth. This symbol, he said, finally contains the "innermost god-like essence of man." It stands for the deity as well as the self since it reflects the image of the godhead in the unfolded creation in nature and in man.

You are not likely to have such lofty thoughts immediately since you are more concerned with the opposites, e.g., you love and resent your children at the same time, or you want to be powerful and independent at the same time you feel yielding, soft, and needy. In order for the process to be effective you must begin where you are.

In creating a mandala you might try it first with paint but you should feel free to make other choices—some people dance them. Jung, when he wanted to reach his creative source not only painted but also played with stones as building blocks. Use whatever material appeals to you. Some illustrations are provided, but *your* mandala will develop in your relating to the particular polarities, opposites that you are attempting to reconcile and understand in your life.

The one essential element to a mandala is a *center.* Symmetry and cardinal points brought into relationship with one another around this center are basic elements but they will vary according to the nature of what is depicted. The mandala will essentially be a vehicle for concentrating your mind so you can relate to apparent contradictions in order to reach a deeper, more inclusive sense of your inner center, the source of your energy, your inner self. For this reason it is important that you take great care and concentration. First find a quiet room or a natural setting, then choose the issue you want to explore, one of the following perhaps.

MANDALA POSSIBILITIES

1. Your day and your night, the different aspects of you that come into awareness with the dawn, the activity of the day, the transition of dusk into evening, and finally the part of you that comes into being with the night.

2. The present year, or your life span from birth to death, or the particular period of your life you are in now.

3. Your body, top and bottom, right and left sides, front and back. Feel and think out your attitudes towards each part.

4. The inner experience of you and your outer relationships with others or of the relationship between your masculine and feminine aspects, your thinking and feeling, and any other division you are aware of.

5. Make a mandala with another person. First, in talking, explore your differences and their relationship to one another; then, in painting, find the colors and symbols to express how each of you experiences yourself in relationship to the other.

Now that you have chosen your issue, center yourself by letting the cares and concerns of the day drop away, concentrate your conscious mind to develop an image of your center. You might close your eyes and envision a blank piece of paper and simply wait. The image which comes might be a flame, a star, a stone, a circle, whatever. When it appears, make that the center of your construction. Now consider the opposites that you are going to work with.

Stay with this as long as necessary to find and simplify the most basic qualities of these opposites. You want to develop a symbolic awareness. You may have begun with the rhythm of a day and a night in your life but when you symbolize them you may find they extend to a basic statement and awareness of life and death. Go with your awareness to as many levels as occur, then again search for the essential symbols to express what you have found. Add these to your mandala, relating them in their dynamic polarity to your existing center.

The dialogue mandala is particularly useful with your marriage partner. So often it is possible to implicitly assume your wife or husband has to think as you do or feel as deeply about something as you do, or you are not understood. Another possibility is that you each need the other to be very much as he/she is to provide a balance and a tension for your growth as an individual. For instance, in doing this exercise, my husband who is quite concrete and specific in his thinking and goal directed, represented himself in the center of the mandala as a diamond-edged, multicolored star. I am more of a goal drifter but oriented to energy and *seeing what wants to*

happen, so I represented myself as a flame sparking out from between and around his edges, a fairly accurate reflection of the problems and richness we hold for one another.

Learning what you are, how you function inside yourself and with those persons closest to you, you are by that very awareness changing yourself. You are becoming more responsive and responsible for the growth of your inner wholeness, finding your inner center which now guides the integration of all that you are. However, there is one further step which involves taking an overview of your whole life span, and for this it is useful to look at life stories, your own and others.

THE WAY IS THE GOAL AND THE GOAL IS THE WAY

Myths, life scripts and your own transformation

Myths are man's attempt to answer *why*? Why are things the way they are and how did they get started? Marie Louise von Franz, a Jungian analyst who has delved deeply into the figures, persons and patterns in fairy tales, suggests that ultimately these tales, too, all tell the same story of man's journey and the different archetypal elements with which he must come to terms. Your interest in looking at these universal stories now is to identify whether they have something specific to say to you about your individual life story.

Eric Berne, in developing Transactional Analysis, outlined a typology in his versions of myths and fairy tales to explain some of the common forms of personal disturbance he observed. He said there are only a limited number of possible ways to live your life, and they have all been capsulized in myth and fairy tale. In working with a patient, he found it useful to relate the patient's life to a coherent story which has survived for hundreds or thousands of years because of its universal appeal to the primitive layers of the human mind. This, at the least, gave him a feeling of working from a solid foundation and, at best, very precise clues as to what needed to be done to avoid a bad ending. An amusing and rueful example he developed is "Sleeping Beauty or Waiting for Rigor Mortis." The story is one of the many myths about a magic sleep. Remember Brunhild left sleeping on the mountain with a ring of fire around her which only the hero Siegfried can penetrate? These myths all contain some of the same elements: a woman caught by the evil spell of another, a long period of sleep cut off from contact with the ordinary world, a hero who overcomes the obstacles or simply comes at the right time, and an awakening.

In "Sleeping Beauty " an angry fairy says that Briar Rose, Sleeping Beauty, will prick her finger with a spindle when she is 15 and will fall down dead. Another fairy commutes this to 100 years of sleep. When she is 15, she does prick her finger, immediately falls asleep, and at the same time everything and everyone else in the castle also falls asleep. During the hundred years, many princes try to reach her, but none succeed until the time is up at last and a prince arrives who finds Briar Rose, kisses her, she wakes, and they fall in love. At the same time, everyone else takes up exactly where they left off as though nothing had happened. The princess herself is still 15 and not 115.

The problem for a present-day heroine living this life story or script is that everything and everybody cannot be unchanged after a lapse of so many years. *This* is the illusion on which the script is based, that modern Rose be 15 years old again instead of 30, 40, or 50 when she wakes up, and that she and the Prince will have a whole lifetime ahead of them. It is hard to tell a real life Rose that princes are younger men and by the time they reach her age, they have become kings, settled down, and are usually much less interested.

This script is also known as "Frigid Woman" because the woman acting it out has often bought the notion that she should not feel sexual, that part of her is sleeping. There is usually an antiscript in which it would be okay if she married the right person, i.e., the Prince with the Golden Apples. A practical problem occurs if she does find the Prince with the Golden Apples. She may feel outclassed and find fault by playing "Blemish" to bring him down to her level, or if she settles for less—the Prince with the Silver Apples, or even ordinary McIntoshes from the grocery store—she will feel cheated and take it out on him while still keeping an eye out for the Golden One.

This script is important because a great many people, one way or another, spend a lifetime waiting for the Prince, the Rescuer, the right job, right opportunity, whatever, instead of waking up to the reality that they individually are responsible for making the condition or quality of their own lives.

Berne's typology of myths and fairy tales pictures the protagonist as blocking, evading, or fearing growth. His treatment aims to recover the original growth impulses, but Berne did not take the next step. He did not identify the myth of the person who achieves wholeness.

A model exists: the journey of the Hero constitutes a universal heritage of mankind. We are probably most familiar with stories like John Bunyan's *Pilgrim's Progress*, or Bible heroes like Joseph who was abandoned by his brothers in jealousy and became the King's advisor in Egypt, or the Greek heroes and heroines, Hercules, Ulysses, Jason of the Golden Fleece, Psyche, Persephone. But all cultures have similar Hero journeys: Beowulf in the Anglo-Saxon, Kiovick in the Eskimo, Parsifal in the German.

Basically, the story starts with the hero in a known but stagnant place. Things were once good in his land but now a sense of blight has taken over and some reparation or restoration has to take place. This he undertakes by starting the journey to the unknown and thus begins a time of trials: he meets his opposites, overcomes dragons and other terrors while keeping his wits about him. Mastering the first trial, he develops strength for the next and sometimes gets a magic potion or amulet from the conquest that will stand him in good stead in later difficulties. There are always several more to come. In the process of his journey, he undergoes a transformation, and when he returns to his land, the missing element is restored and he is recognized as the Hero, the one who completed the task. The land is healed.

My view of the hero is not as the exceptional man (although at present there may be relatively few self-actualizing men) but rather as that unfolding potential in every person which can be unblocked. Every person undertakes a journey when he begins to consciously accept responsibility for his own choices. What shall I do with today? What shall I do with my life? How can I deal with my anxiety, aggression, and hostility? How shall I meet these feelings in others? How can I use my sexuality fully and creatively? What does personal integrity demand? What meaning is there in the word *God?* Choices in answer to questions like these orient the beginning quest.

Your story is largely determined by the situation into which you are born, and you stagnate until a certain degree of consciousness awakens usually through a crisis—a death, divorce, loss of an important goal—or perhaps the recognition that you just don't fit your context, something you would never have chosen. You are forced down into what feels like emptiness and often despair. After a time you begin to grope in the darkness, looking for some way out. Perhaps you enter therapy, perhaps you do it on your own. But with this first step you begin the upward ascent. You begin your journey.

Jeremy, the young lawyer whose family sculpture we considered, was thinking of divorce until it occurred to him that his sense of not fitting was much broader than just his relation to his wife. The pervasiveness of his sense of boredom and lack of meaning initially felt to him like a tight prison with no way out. Paradoxically, that is the turning point. Only by realizing the full darkness and emptiness he had been avoiding, could he begin to ask the right questions. Why am I living the way I am, what are the possible choices I did not acknowledge, what were their costs, is it too much to pay to become my *own man?*

The time of trials takes you through peaks and valleys of feeling, down and up until you reach a point at which everything is seen in a new light. You then become conscious of the underlying purposiveness in your life, particularly of the darkness that you regarded as evil. If Jeremy hadn't fallen into a depression, he would have continued to exist half alive. So the evil, the depression, was the way out. Some describe this recognition as satori, others as enlightenment, still others as individuation. It is not an end point. The journey goes on.

One such Hero tale, cited by analysts Elizabeth Howes and Sheila Moon in *Man the Choicemaker* is that of Sir Gawain and Lady Ragnell. Gawain, one of King Arthur's finest knights, in order to save the life of his beloved king, agreed to marry a loathsome lady with a hideous face and great twisting eyes. She seemed to be enormously greedy and fat and sat hunched on her horse like a great bale of straw. Gawain kept his promise although the court shuddered with horror. On their wedding night, Gawain kissed her and afterward wept in agony, but at that instant, Ragnell, who had been enchanted, was freed and became her young and beautiful self—but for only half each twenty-four hour period. Gawain must choose, she said, did he want her beautiful by night and repellant by day, or the other way around? Gawain answered, "With you is the greatest suffering, and you alone must choose what you are most able to bear." With this final sacrifice, the enchantment completely lifted. What he offered up was enormous, the humiliating sacrifice of his own desires for the sake of the Round Table and its safety. What he received back was more—his king's life preserved, the security of the Round Table, and an unexpected love.

In a group discussing this tale of sacrifice and redemption and making it more personally relevant, one man might remark all choice inevitably involves sacrifice. In order to develop any relationship with another, some personal autonomy has to be given up. Another person's first thought is how preconceptions have to be let go in the process of creating an original work. A third comments that for the sake of psychological growth, favorite self images and defenses have to be laid aside.

A theme gradually develops of how we shun and are reluctant to relate to the darker aspects of ourselves because we are so unwilling to give up our favorite points of view and our onesided images. But all sacrifice is not redemptive! Look at the people who play martyr and victim games. Clearly there are two kinds of sacrifice, one egocentric in its manipulative desire to be praised and loved, and the other a letting go *to* something which is of greater value. In the tale, the greater value was the life of the king and the security of the Round Table, that great symbol of wholeness.

Excerpts from a journal:

3 February 1972: *I am experiencing another self that I have not been in touch with. I feel the greatest need to SEE that other self and make contact.*

8 May 1972: *I have entered the valley of the Shadow of Death. I am feeling despair, not that I can't go on, but yes that I must go on. The tree in the foreground is living but the dead tree in the distance tells me that I am coming to a place where something in me must die so that something else can be born.*

22 December 1972: *Everything is blue in this painting. I have moved from a world of red hot heat into water. I feel tranquil and peaceful. The man inside and the woman inside me are together on the raft and moving towards the horizon where the edge of the sun appears. It seems to me that the Sun which can't be fully seen yet is centered on this page and is my own wholeness.*

Each participant now considers for himself alone, either in writing or using art media to focus his attention. Who or what is Ragnell to me? To what aspect of my life does she correspond? What feels grotesquely deformed and hideous in myself that I must relate to? One woman may find her reflections leading in the direction of a current struggle she is facing between choosing to stay in a stable and good but endlessly tepid marriage or giving it up for a new relationship which promises to be richly creative. She does not wish to hurt her husband whom she genuinely cares for but she does not want to lose this new meaning. What is she to do? Shall she renounce the new and struggle with the old? Shall she work with the new meanings only inside herself? What is the larger value which needs to be rescued? Another person might find his Ragnell to be a long buried hostility that has at last been uncovered. How should he relate to it? Hold on to it, let go of it, express it, work with it in some other way? Each person struggling with these questions has to risk his individual decisions. He has to renounce his old dependence on outer authority but his self respect and personal strength grows.

There are two ways to work with myths. One used by the Guild for Psychological Studies in San Francisco starts with an actual myth, e.g., the Legends of the Grail. Usually two leaders work with the texts and the group in a Socratic dialogue that enables each participant to take the story inward and relate it to the personal content of his life. Later, in working alone with art materials, each person develops the symbols most meaningful for him personally. Sharing these in a later group session deepens the experience for all.

The following method is a way of discovering your personal myth. I use it with both individuals and groups.

WRITING YOUR MYTH

Write the story of your life as a myth. What is your mythic name? What was the event or crisis that started you on your journey? Who are your companions and how did you meet? You might personify your dark self as well as your inner man or inner woman. What was the land like from which you started? Where did you go? Who and what did you encounter? Then what happened?

Cassie, an ex-nun living alone and working at a bookkeeping job that in no way reflected her abilities, took no initiative in establishing a social life and put down attempts by others to get to know her. From her dreams and fantasies, she identified a cast of characters within her: a crying baby she despised; a small, red, angry child; a critic analyst also known as the executioner; and a totally inept mediator who was the designated leader but who felt helpless when the others fought. I had her imagine them starting out on a journey together, what they would each bring, and how they would manage various obstacles.

By understanding her myth, she found that the crying child actually had a strong ability to judge what possibilities and situations would feel right for all of the group to explore, she did not cry at all when interested and taken care of. The angry red child was male, had independence, strength, and more than a streak of the adventurer in him; he scouted territory and found and made bridges over dangerous chasms. The critic was nasty but also a very good computer-navigator and by the end had developed his own brand of vinegary humor, a quite tolerable companion indeed. We were now able to look for the strengths in her. She could acknowledge them as her own.

Now you have some direction. You have formed some images of the place you stand and from where you start. You have some navigation instruments, your dreams and active imagination, and from your inner explorings you have begun a tentative map. You need time alone now to discover your inner aspects, how you need to nourish them and continue your journey. A time to be inwardly attentive is essential to the growth of those small beginnings, the gathering together of meaning.

As one who makes the inward journey, you come to see outer reality more accurately, unscreened and free from distortions of your projections and wants. You know you can find and react to all sorts of symbols, from inside as in your dreams and from outside in the outer events and persons who enter your life. Broader than that, you can find your connection to the very cosmos itself. Recent discoveries in astronomy, physics, biology, paleontology, and geology show a complex web of relationships between ourselves, our planet, our solar system, our galaxy, with one another and the universe that gave birth to us all. Just as when you looked at the collected wisdom in myths for parallels to understand your own journey towards wholeness, you can also find similar parallels in the objective scientific story of the formation of simple chemical compounds, the growth of organic molecules, the development of living tissue to the capacity for self awareness. Von Ditfurth in his *Children of the Universe*, Teilhard de Chardin in *The Phenomenon of Man*, Loren Eiseley, Fred Hoyle, Rachel Carson—these are a few of the scientists who place our inward journey in the wonderous context of a continuing story. You alone, however, can relate the two worlds, inner and outer, choosing, persevering, bringing together many opposites, sacrificing the self images that act as barriers to understanding. And nothing feeds this process so much as creative work. Although I use art forms in therapy, my aim is not solely to point to these as potentially fulfilling pursuits in themselves but as tools to open up for consideration

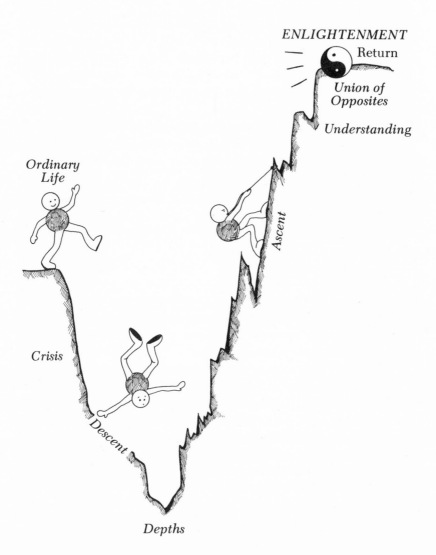

ENLIGHTENMENT

Return

*Union of
Opposites*

Understanding

*Ordinary
Life*

Ascent

Crisis

Descent

Depths

JOURNEY OF THE HERO

the many possibilities of the inner life that have not been explored and can be expressed in creative action.

Susanne K. Langer says it well in an essay on "The Growing Center of Knowledge":

> Only a small part of reality for a human being is what is actually going on; the greater part is what he imagines in connection with the sights and sounds of the moment.... This is not to say his life is a dream, his world a fantasy or any such pseudo-philosophical thing. It means that his world is bigger than the stimuli that surround him and the measure of it is in the reach of his steady and coherent imagination. An animal's environment consists of things that act on his senses....a human being's world hangs together. Its events fit into each other; no matter how devious their connections, in one big framework of time and space.... The world is something human. *

That getting a sense of "how my world hangs together" is essential. You need to give yourself time for the thoughtful going inward, time for a deeper connection with your surroundings and senses as well as the imaginative consideration of possible options, the wonderful "what if's" you can consider, then choose, in developing and allowing your multifaceted self to be.

---

*Susanne K. Langer, "The Growing Center of Knowledge," *Philosophical Sketches*. Baltimore: John Hopkins Press, 1962, pp. 145–6.

MAPS
AND
CHARTS

II

THE CREATIVE PROCESS

Creativity lies in the discovery of unsuspected links. Before the new possibilities emerge, however, there is usually a period of massive discomfort. In my experience as a psychotherapist, this crisis and feelings of anger, pain, boredom, and self-dissatisfaction that originally brings a person into psychotherapy, often correspond to the first stage of a profoundly creative process. The individual able to proceed beyond this stage will achieve greater awareness and solutions to the personal problems that confront him.

Clearing away the obstacles to this process consists largely of helping the individual to discover his present autonomy and unacknowledged power. Transactional Analysis is one of the tools used to guide to this discovery. TA offers quick, effective methods for identifying the decisions an individual has made in the light of his early life situation, decisions that currently distort his perceptions and ability to meet his present needs.

In applying the framework of TA to their problems, some people find the gimmicky language and apparent oversimplification obstructive. Initially this is how it seemed to me when I was studying with Eric Berne 20 years ago. His succinct restatement of the essence of Freudian theory, group dynamics, and what we then knew of social psychology, I recognized as elegant if unorthodox, but the feelings and emotions of the client did not seem to matter enough. Something was missing in the gamey *nothing but* explanations of behavior. A woman may play "If It Weren't for You" to hide her doubts of her own ability and reluctance to accept the discipline of a career. Defining the game helps her to face these issues; however, it may block seeing her behavior as proceeding from any other level of meaning, e.g., the interplay of values between her creative power and her destructive anger, that within her which pushes for transformation.

The Gestalt approach of Fritz Perls added an essential dimension to my knowledge—the living here and now experience of the client with his full feeling complexity, the various elements within his person warring and struggling to be recognized. TA and Gestalt combine to form powerful tools for understanding behavior. The woman in a Gestalt experience of her game "If It Weren't for You" enacts her projection of her husband's constraint, then her talent struggling to be free. She feels strongly this polarization within her and, in attempting to form a bridge between them, she uncovers and owns the value they represent.

What was now missing was something I had not previously included in psychology—the *meaning* in a person's life, the sense of being more than we can account for that struggles for expression in what we aspire to be and do. Jung's writings gave some indication of the importance of this *meaning*, but I didn't immediately realize the *means* for understanding the more than was here. During Jungian analysis with Joseph Wheelwright, I discovered art methods with collage brought me into touch with aspects of self which had a reality beyond the confines which I had previously thought of as *myself*. The process I was beginning is one common to artists, musicians, scientists, actors, but also to preschoolers absorbed in finger painting and high schoolers struggling to write a theme paper.

There is a phase of uneasiness, of sensing that something wants to happen, then an exploring and manipulating of some material, finding out about the elements of it, the possibilities, combinations and patterns, ways of doing and using. There are phases of frustration and a need to get away from it and turn our conscious thoughts to something else, but we keep being drawn back. Suddenly, there it is. The elements have come together in a pattern and we are almost flooded with what wants to come out, what wants to be expressed. We *see* what we had not seen before.

There seems to be an aspect within each of us that, if given sufficient material, will begin to organize in patterns that express something of its otherwise unseeable self. By analogy, this is like scattering iron filings on a paper over a magnet. Each iron particle reacts to the magnetic field, becoming magnetized by induction, attracting or repelling the other nearby granules, all of which become organized into a pattern corresponding to the magnetic field of the underlying magnet. We then see a pattern on the paper which represents intense magnetization, the lines of force of the otherwise invisible field. This aspect within us serves as a magnetic field, developing materials in patterns of creative purpose.

The work we do with material and thought provides the stimulus. Then when we let go with our efforts, the influence of the creative field begins to intensify. The preparation we do provides the basic elements with which the creative field plays. Our creative aspect selects those elements which correspond most closely to its own patterns and contributes insight to our problem. The incubation stage during which the creative field develops and is expressed without conscious manipulation can last from a few seconds to many years. Some of the patterns which recur time after time correspond remarkably to universal symbols that are found in myths, fairy tales, art, and literature of all cultures. They also recur in the dreams and art processes of the person looking inward at his own consciousness. They are partially what Jung identified as the archetypes, inherited experiences unconscious in the present individual. Recently astronomers, paleontologists, physicists and other scientists have discovered similar patterns in the cosmos, linking processes occurring in the formation of the stars to the formation of organic molecules through the development of our own self-reflective awareness. When we experience and try out new meanings we are deeply involved with the very stuff of the cosmos.

The growth process of connecting with all that we are capable of being resumes when we stop limiting ourselves and unlock some of the energy used to do the limiting. I consider the theories of TA, Gestalt, and Jungian psychology to be integrally related. They are like charts and maps. TA can clear the ground and provide much of the preparation, Gestalt unblocks the emotional power, and Jungian thought provides a sense of direction.

Transactional Analysis (TA) began when Eric Berne observed a man change his tone of voice, his facial expression, and his gestures. In the course of a relatively few minutes, he was a whining little boy, then switched to acting like a stern judgmental parent even to shaking his fist. Finally he changed to a reflective adult computing some changes in his business that had to be made. Berne concluded that each of us operates from three basically different ego states. These are characterized by different feelings, actions, types of decisions, body postures, and gestures.

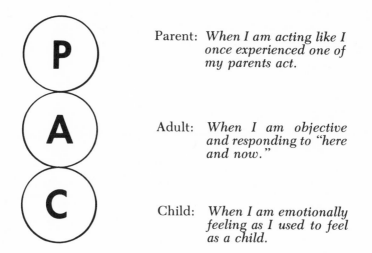

Parent: *When I am acting like I once experienced one of my parents act.*

Adult: *When I am objective and responding to "here and now."*

Child: *When I am emotionally feeling as I used to feel as a child.*

When in a *Parent* state of mind the person embodies actual sets of feelings, values, maxims, and judgments that he once experienced coming from one of his parents. He may literally use the tone of voice or gestures that his parent used to put over his point of view.

When in a *Child* ego state he is operating with the feelings, drives, and needs that he actually experienced in childhood.

In the *Adult* ego state he is present-centered, in touch with the situation in which he finds himself. He is making decisions and acting with a real here and now response to what the situation calls for. This is in contrast to the Parent response which characteristically is a should or ought type of judgment failing to compute relevant information that had not been available or would have been ignored by the original parent. The Adult state response differs from the Child in computing consequences rationally rather than acting from a feeling or need response.

In growing up, each child makes *Decisions* that largely determine the kind of life he is going to lead. These are made in response to his experiences but particularly in response to certain messages he receives from his parents. Bear in mind that each parent has three ego states too, so some of their messages may come from a hurt, confused, inadequate, or frightened Child that has limited them and which they pass on to their children.

Injunctions: Don'ts and Dos

Injunctions are comprised of all the messages received from the Child part of the parents. These messages tend to be the *Don'ts* and are sometimes deadly, e.g., *Don't be (Don't exist)*, from the woman who did not want a child and viewed it as an interference with what she did want. Sometimes the parent has wanted a child of the opposite sex, and the child gets the message *Don't be a girl*, or *Don't be a boy*. Often when the parent has failed to achieve something he/she wanted, the child gets the message, *Don't be you (Be my ideal self)*. The messages are given verbally and nonverbally, directly and indirectly, e.g., *I'm cold; go put on your sweater, Johnny. You're not hungry yet; you're just tired*, eventually gets translated: *Don't feel what you feel; feel what I feel.*

Sometimes when tears and anger are not acceptable, the child gets the message, *Don't feel* or *Don't be a child.* Occasionally something in the parent is threatened if the child is too talented or too successful and *Don't make it* or *Don't be important* are sent. Other messages are *Don't be well* or *Don't be sane* and sometimes just *Don't (Whatever you're doing, stop it).*

From the Parent ego state of the parent comes other messages about what would please the parent, make the child acceptable, and what behaviors will be rewarded. TA calls attention of any kind *stroking;* the child can work for positive (approval) or negative (punishment) strokes, the latter on the theory that any attention is better than none. The Parent instructions tend to be worded as such: *Work hard; Be a lady; Make good grades; Be strong; Be unselfish; Be obedient: Be seen but not heard; Be popular; Be kind; Be perfect.*

Just as a child easily learns the native language of his country and this language shapes his perceptions, things he recognizes as important, each family has it's own emotional language which determines the Injunctions and which emotional experience the child will recognize as important. A child whose early experience of women is bossy and domineering will later be more highly aware of bossy domineering traits in women than another whose experience of women was of a gentle and submissive mother.

Decisions

While the messages received from parents make up the child's *Injunctions,* his *Decisions* are made to buy or not to buy the Injunctions based on the kind of stress in which he finds himself and the ways he sees to get strokes he needs to survive in this given place and this given time. The problem comes when these early Decisions have been carried forward and the present day situation is not the same, e.g., the man has physical power and freedom to determine his choices that the child did not possess but he can still be acting out of an ego state that feels powerless.

Some of the problematic Decisions the child can make are:

> *I'll show you, even if it kills me.*
>
> *If things don't go right, I'll kill myself.*
>
> *I'll get you, even if it kills me.*
>
> *I'll do the things the other sex does. . . and I'll be lonely.*
>
> *I'll show you I can be a boy/girl.*
>
> *I'll never really make it.*
>
> *I'll succeed but I won't enjoy it.*
>
> *I'll never let anyone know my real feelings (I'll hide my feelings).*
>
> *I'm no good.*
>
> *It does not pay (work) to put myself first.*

Anna's situation used in family sculpting illustrates the interplay between Injunctions, Decisions, and Redecisions. Adult Redecisions based on current reality and not programmed by the past can be made when the underlying pattern of Injunctions, Decisions, Rackets, Games, and Scripting is apparent.

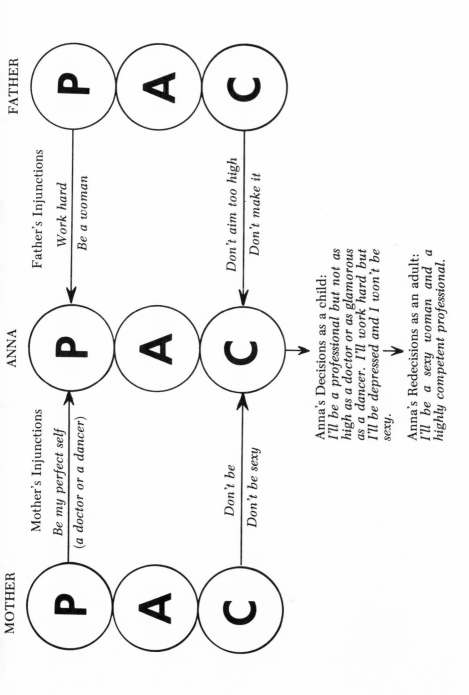

MOTHER   ANNA   FATHER

Mother's Injunctions   Father's Injunctions

Be my perfect self   *Work hard*

(a doctor or a dancer)   *Be a woman*

Don't be   *Don't aim too high*

Don't be sexy   *Don't make it*

Anna's Decisions as a child:
I'll be a professional but not as high as a doctor or as glamorous as a dancer. I'll work hard but I'll be depressed and I won't be sexy.

Anna's Redecisions as an adult:
I'll be a sexy woman and a highly competent professional.

Rackets

Rackets in TA terminology refer to a person's chronic negative stereotyped feeling reaction to stress. Some people seem to be chronically angry, others depressed, others confused. A Racket gets started in the early family situation when one or more feelings are highly unacceptable. In Anna's family it was not O.K. to feel either sexy or to feel angry, so instead of having those forbidden feelings when they were called for, Anna would feel sad and powerless which was acceptable and even got some stroking in the form of attention.

Racket feelings are substitutes for the true feeling called for in a situation. When the true feeling is identified, it calls for an action to achieve the underlying need. The feeling is then discharged and the person moves on to meet the next emerging situation. He is not hung up with any particular feeling. A Racket feeling on the other hand is never on target so the real need is not identified and taken care of. The person continues to collect the Racket feeling because it is not discharged; it does not meet the underlying need.

Games

Games, as defined by TA, are ways of interacting with others (or in one's own head) that end up with Racket feelings. They start with an ostensibly straight message to the other person's Adult but this contains a secret message to the other's Child or Parent state. The secret message is responded to and the initiator collects his *old familiar feeling.*

One of the easiest games to recognize is "Why Don't You Yes But" first described by Eric Berne: One player, who is *it*, presents a problem. The others start to present solutions each beginning with, *Why don't you. . .* The one who is *it* objects with a *Yes, but. . .* A good player can stand off the rest of the group indefinitely until they all give up, whereupon *it* wins.

The ostensible purpose, an Adult quest for information, contains a secret message from the Child, *I'm inadequate to meet this situation*, designed to hook the other person's sage Parent, anxious to dispense wisdom, which is exactly what *it* wants since her object is to confound these Parents one after the other. As the game ends, all those who offered advice are dejected, having failed to help and *it* has proved the point that her problem is really insoluble which makes it possible for her to indulge herself in her Racket feeling of depression and self-pity.

The real feeling, which was masked, is anger originally based on a situation of powerlessness, vis-a-vis her original parents. To break up the Game, another person can simply respond from his Adult which does not automatically accept the *I am a powerless child* secret bait, e.g., *Oh, really? What have you tried?*, and if it becomes clear that *it* will not give up the Game and acknowledge her Adult power to find her own solutions, the other adult can either confront her with her Game or move on to more interesting topics of conversation.

Victims, Persecutors, and Rescuers

Game participants have three positions to play from: *Victim, Persecutor*, or *Rescuer*. In the course of the Game these get switched, e.g., in "Why Don't You Yes But" the initiator originally starts as a helpless Victim of the terrible problem and invites someone to be Rescuer. As the Game ends it becomes apparent that he has been persecuting the others and they are Victims of the Game.

I differ from most Transactional Analysts in that I view the essence of a *Game* or set of *Games* a person chooses as an inner flirtation with a core life question, a psychological value imposed by the early Injunctions. This always takes the form of an impasse in which both alternatives are equally feared. The Game insures that neither is faced.

For Anna the core Injunction was *Don't Be*. It took the form of a life question, *Am I wanted or not wanted?* In early school she learned to play "Gee Whiz, Professor, You're Wonderful—You're Unusually Perceptive." She successfully masked her differences of thought and feeling from a succession of male mentors, and avoided the possibility of being seen and valued (with the burden of defining her own position) as well as the possibility of being really seen and rejected. Later with her husband and children she played "Harried." She agreed with all their criticism, accepted all their demands, expected herself to function perfectly as a housekeeper, interior decorator, cook, mother, wife, *and* she said yes to everything extra that was asked of her at work, which occasionally justified a complete collapse (when a critical task would not be done and she caused others to be heavily *let down*). The basic motif was *If I do everything for you, surely you'll want me (but you wouldn't want me if you knew how angry I am)*.

Obviously to play a Game you have to find other people who are willing to play their parts for their own purposes. Selecting partners is much like casting for a play, a few rehearsals determine suitability. What follows is much like a theatrical event: a prescribed cast of characters, dialogue, acts and scenes, themes and plots which can move to a dramatic climax and end with a final curtain or, alternatively, can peter on endlessly like a TV soap opera, going nowhere.

Life Script

The *Life Script*, a TA term for a person's ongoing program for his life, dictates where he is going and how he is going to get there. It is a drama he compulsively acts although his awareness of it may be vague. The man who has taken the position that you can't trust women, marries a sequence of women who let him down. He fulfills his prophecy by selecting a girl who has some indicated potential for nontrust, then he pushes her into situations of trial, complains, becomes jealous, and generally makes life miserable so that eventually she proves his point that *you can't trust women* by taking off with someone else. The woman who marries a series of alcoholics is doing the same thing.

The complementary nature of Scripting in marriage selection can again be illustrated by Anna who selected a man who would never really reassure her that she was wanted or clearly reject her. He seemed totally absorbed in his job as executive in an expanding company. He in turn was in an impasse felt most acutely in his work life, whether or not he had the power to make it to the top. Really dealing with either of these alternatives felt catastrophic to him. If he made it to the top, he would have the burden of constantly proving his ability to stay there, the tension of dealing with other men's envy, and the felt danger of their aggressive competition. If he allowed himself to feel that he did not have the ability (power) to get to the top, he would feel depressed, empty, and suicidal. His major parental Injunction had been *Don't make it*. His Child's decision had been *I'll show you even if it kills me*. The Games he played to avoid resolving the impasse were mostly variants of "If It Weren't for You" although he played his own version of "Harried." Just as his wife tended to project and hear her parental Injunctions as now coming from him, so too he tended to project and hear the *Don't make it* message coming from her and used it to build up, justify, and collect angry feelings (covering the true feeling of fear and anxiety) which made a realistic assessment of his ability unlikely.

Redecisions

Treatment involves analyzing ego states, transactions, Games, Injunctions, Decisions, and Scripts. The core, however, involves one thing to get through the impasse, making a Redecision.

If the person recognizes that he made a wrong Decision at some point in his early life then he can change that Decision. He cannot give up his Injunctions until he stops shifting responsibility, until he lets his parents go, recognizing that they were real people suffering their own disappointments and hurts and passing some of them on, which he can now forgive. He can know the Redecisions that have to be made either by doing the Family Sculpture, or by fantasizing where he will be ten years from now if he continues to follow his Script, and where he will be if he makes a different Decision.

Then he can really begin to change, to stop playing Games, to stop maintaining his Rackets, to stop following his Life Script, and to become autonomous. The real success comes when the client carries out his Redecision to enjoy life, to live, when he no longer denies or restricts his autonomy. He uses different language. He says *I* when he means *I* instead of beginning statements with *You* or *One* or *We*. He says *he won't*, when he means *won't* instead of copping out under words like *try, can't, want, should* and the *why-because* rationalizations. He begins to experience the joy of being free and learns there are other more satisfying kinds of strokes for changing that come from his experience of being himself.

Gestalt techniques focus on awareness and self responsibility in the present moment. Fritz Perls found that people blocked their awareness, their experience of the present by ruminating about the past or fantasizing about the future. He observed that people who seemed more alive and free from anxiety were very much in touch with their current experiencing, met each situation flexibily as it arose. Their responses were spontaneous, required little effort yet seemed centered in some way.

Perls decided this centeredness in the present moment could best be explained by the old German notion of *gestalt* or the pattern of figure and ground. The healthy person is in touch with his own needs either as they arise from within (a need to urinate, a feeling of hunger, or sexual tension) or as opportunities develop outside for the satisfaction of longer term interests and capacities for enjoyment, e.g., he relishes the beauty of a garden or of teaching his child a new skill. These needs and longer term interests and capacities for enjoyment affect his perception of the present moment in a distinct way. The emerging need organizes his field of awareness so the opportunities to meet the need stand out, e.g., the hungry man picks up the aroma of food, the sight of food, and is aware of opportunities to eat. These stimuli become the foreground of his interest until he eats and the rest recedes to the background. Now, however, having satisfied his hunger, his perceptions shift in response to whatever next occupies his interest and the food items recede to the background.

Aside from the body needs of hunger, discharge of wastes, and sexual arousal, Perls observed that most people were in meager contact with their experiences, only half awake to reality. In fact, even with the body needs some people do not do so well. A man can eat automatically, not in response to hunger. He may have sex without enjoyment or, alternatively, be out of touch with sexual hunger. He is either unaware of his specific needs or blocked in demanding what he wants. Often he does not know how to ask or is confused about what he really wants. But once he can express his demands, his requests directly and actually mean what he says, he has made the most important step in feeling his own worth.

Perls defined learning as discovering that something is possible. He said it was possible to discover means and ways to grow but we use most of our energies for self-destructive, self-preventing games because we run away from the unpleasant and the painful. Mostly what we are running from is hurt to our vanity. We do not like to look at that nor at when we feel hurt, we also actually feel vindictive and want to hurt the other person.

So we turn our attention to other things. You can either be in touch with the world, in touch with yourself, or in touch with your fantasy life. When fantasies are taken for a real thing, that is insanity. In our fantasy zone are the catastrophic expectations that distort our view of the world and keep us from meeting our needs simply. But there is also a fantasy of who we are, a self concept that gives us no support. On the contrary, we use it to nag, disapprove, and squash much of our genuine self-expression and along with this we look for approval, affection from others that we won't give ourselves.

One source of confusion between our real self and self-concept is that often we think we should feel either/or, that we should feel love or hate, that we are good or bad. We merely have to replace this with both/and to make it clear that the positive or negative depends on a context. This is much like Jungian psychology's emphasis on the identification and integration of opposites necessary to become an individual.

Gestalt does not provide long explanations of *why* we are as we are. There are no scapegoats to blame. Like giving up the TA Game of "Wooden Leg," we can no longer say *How can you expect me to be any different when I had such a rotten childhood?* Instead, Gestalt has one prescription: Take responsibility; experience yourself as the doer of your actions; stop avoiding, covering up your experience; experience *you*.

Only through integrated spontaniety and deliberateness can we make sound choices. Awareness of our responsibility for the whole field, for the self as well as the other, gives meaning and pattern to our individual life.

Techniques to Stop Avoiding

There are two types of techniques that bring more direct contact with present experiences: One to stop avoiding and the other to intensify attention or exaggerate the experience. These techniques involve stopping the activities that keep us so busy we hardly have any attention left for the moment we are living. There is little place for the *now* in ordinary conversation. We tell stories, share opinions and plans. Even our private mental activity is mostly anticipations, memories, fantasies, and fitting games. Many of these activities emerge in our art experiences indicating how they pervade all aspects of living.

Aboutism. This is what Perls used to call the "Science" Game. He considered the *whys* and *because* of talk most often as rationalization, sheer verbiage, and unsubstantial when weighed against direct experience. Tabooing this type of intellectualizing serves to bring to light what lies hidden behind it, often a sense of emptiness and impotence. Staying with the emptiness, minor feelings begin to evolve like sparks growing into fires. In art experiences of facing the empty sheet of paper until something grows inside that impels expression, it is possible to contact this inner emptiness without words.

Shouldism. Telling ourselves or others what should be is another way of not experienceing what *is*. Evaluating means fitting this now experience to our preestablished standards. We attend to what is missing rather than what is present and often create the unpleasant feelings of frustration rather than awareness of what there is to grasp. In giving up *should*, we stop self-blaming and self-praising. The sign, means, and goal are

determined when we can simply acknowledge experience without justifying or criticising. In each art exercise, the person's unique expression of his experience is what it is. There is no way it could be *better*.

If we look carefully, we find feelings such as anxiety, guilt, and shame are not direct experiences but the outcome of a mental process. Behind every guilt is the ideal into which we are failing to fit (I should have done a better job; I should be Picasso not me); behind every anxiety, the desire to manipulate the future as we think it should be (You should admire how clever I am).

A goal is a target, a landmark for our orientation, which may be an ideal or not. Gestalt does not seek to eliminate conception of the desirable. It tries to counter an excess of future orientation with good anchorage in the present. *Shoulds* on the other hand oppose a reality that cannot be other than what it is. When we blame ourselves for something past, we do not change the wrongness we concurred in nor is this blaming necessary to do better in the future. Similarly our experiences here and now are what they are; self-blame and self-praise do not change them.

A realistic appraisal of where we are in terms of our aims and ideals is only possible when our evaluation is not biased by the self-punishing game or counteractive defenses. The self-putdown into which we put so much of our energy is altogether different from the serene perception of our failings. The sane attitude towards our failings is similar to that of a good teacher or coach. "That was too high," a tennis coach will say, "Pay attention to your footwork; relax your shoulder more." This takes for granted that you want to use these observations and is very different from demand, manipulation, or control.

Gestalt therapy calls *top-dog* what TA identifies as the Parent ego state. Neither implies that the state should be done away with, only that the state is usually experienced as an imposition of one part of the personality on another. The opposite role is the *underdog* for Gestalt, the Child for TA. Their opposition, whether experienced as an internal battle or whether we manage to induce another person to play one of the opposites, keeps us stuck. The solution in TA and Gestalt is the same as it is in the Jungian approach. We have to identify both aspects as belonging to us. When the opposites are identified, it is possible to assimilate them. *I want* and *I choose* can replace *I should.* The art exercises to identify the opposites of the way we usually think and feel are designed to clarify this inner opposition and make choice possible.

Manipulation

Just as *aboutism* is a misuse of the intellect and *shouldism* is a misuse of the emotions, *manipulation* is a misuse in the sphere of action. For most people, most actions are to avoid a sense of emptiness. One common form of manipulation is to ask questions. Questions not only mask the experience of the questioner but also serve to *suck in* the other to answer and satisfy the questioner's manipulative need. They deviate the content of group interaction away from what is useful. The Gestaltist says, "Make your question into a statement."

Asking for permission is a similar device. Here the individual manipulates the situation so the other takes responsibility for his action and thus the manipulator avoids an impasse, the polarity of his freedom and the fear he feels associated with it. In art therapy all comments by any member of the group on another's work are made using the first person, present tense, and active voice to encourage the members to own their projections and to be responsible for them, and the personal questions they raise.

Expressive and Exaggeration Techniques

In suppressing the cliches, conditioned responses, and games, we become aware of what we are behind these automatic reactions. Exaggerating the expression of impulses heightens awareness of self. Translating your feeling and understanding into words, actions, and forms in art media focuses this sense of aliveness. Expression of a thought, image, or feeling allows an integration of that which was disowned, disassociated from awareness, and therefore ineffective.

The Gestaltist pays close attention to language. He does not allow disowning words, like *it*, *you*, or *we* when the person means *I*. He doesn't accept *can't* when *won't* is meant. *But* is all too often used to disqualify a statement or to take away some of its force: *Yes, but...; I like you, but...; I'd like to do this but...* In this ambiguity, the individual avoids fully experiencing either half of his statement and each invalidates the other. The Gestaltist then suggests instead using *and. I like you AND I'm annoyed by your timidity* allows a stronger encounter.

The individual is confronted with his own choices to the extent a situation is unstructured. Whatever he does, *he* does.

He chooses to follow or not to follow the dictates of his impulses, wishes, leanings of the moment. The function of the Gestaltist is to make him aware of his own decisions, i.e., he is responsible.

Patient: I am holding my jaw very tight. I feel like screaming.

Therapist: And that you are *not* doing.

Patient: I am afraid it would be ridiculous.

Therapist: It?

Patient: I would feel ridiculous doing such a thing.

Therapist: So here you are in conflict—to scream or to fear the group's opinion.

The conflicts most often manifested are between human needs on the one hand and social roles of behavior and consideration of other people's reactions on the other. Smearing paint and working with clay often evoke impulses unacceptable to the present day adult. Articulating them reopens issues of choice.

Sometimes when the Gestaltist wishes to stimulate initiative and risk-taking, he will suggest *gibberish*, unstructured vocalization. It implies a willingness to say the unknown, the unthought. In its lack of structure there is something that molds itself to our inner reality. Sometimes the person may censor all anger from his words, voice, and awareness and yet produce gibberish that is angry beyond a doubt. When a husband and wife are interacting with gibberish, a range of feelings, pleading, arrogance, may be easily apparent that forms a basic substratum to their relationship. Similarly questions and use of control, power, and initiative are obvious in the unstructured use of paint in a dialogue painting between two people.

Reversal

Reversal assumes that the opposite to what is consciously expressed is also likely to be a part of the person, but a less developed side—attitudes, feelings, physical posture in art, the minor aspect of a painting—when reversed and allowed expression, unfolds unsuspected possibilities and experiences. This is very closely allied again to the Jungian notion of identification and assimilation of the opposites within the personality. When the minister's wife identified with her collage of Raquel Welch as the Roller Derby Queen, this was a reversal which allowed unexpected responses.

One particular type of reversal which Perls emphasized had to do with *retroflection*. This is behavior by which a person does to himself what he originally did or tried to do to other persons or objects. He substitutes himself as the target now because he earlier learned that he could not express those impulses outwardly. He actively holds them back, even from his own awareness, but they get a partial discharge in being turned inward. This is somewhat akin to the TA notion of Rackets which are used to elicit familiar bad feelings but cover up an inner feeling which if owned and allowed discharge would finish the situation. The content varies from person to person. Self-hate, self-pity, self-control, even introspection, Perls considered retroflective peering at oneself and different from genuine self-awareness because observer is split off from the part observed.

In undoing this, the person is asked to translate his self-accusations and guilt into resentment statements, his feelings of being ridiculed into sarcasm directed outward, his feeling of having no right to exist into the hate and anger that lies within. This often can be enacted in psychodrama or mime movement before it can be worded as such.

Finishing situations refers to a person's sense of not completing an act. Words unsaid and things undone leave a trace, binding us to the past. Sometimes this involves a psychodrama, acting a fantasy out, finishing an unfinished dream, saying to parents what was not said to them in childhood, saying goodbye to a divorced spouse or dead relative. What was unsaid, withheld, may have been appreciation or resentment.

A similar phenomenon involves *completing expression.* Nonverbal gesture, tears, and sounds can be translated by giving them a voice. First the gesture is exaggerated, made broader or more precise, more intensively expressive of whatever the initial feeling was. It is then translated: "What is your left hand saying as it squeezes your arm? If your tears could speak, what would they say?" In making the content more explicit, the person contacts his message for himself from the inside. Similarly with the images of a dream or a painting or clay sculpture. In acting them out and giving them voice, we *know* more because being something or someone deepens awareness far more than reasoning about it or him.

These little playlets, or skits as Perls called them, form a major way of owning that which was disassociated and projected, and healing the inner splits within the personality. They bring about the end goal of Gestalt: awareness and self-responsibility in the here and now.

If present-centered here and now awareness is the essence of Gestalt psychology, the catch phrase for depth psychology might be: the beginning of self-knowledge is discovery that I am not only that which I identify myself as being but also that which I strenuously reject (plus much more). The accompanying diagram *THE WHOLE PERSON* pictures the relationship between my conscious mind and the rest of what I am.

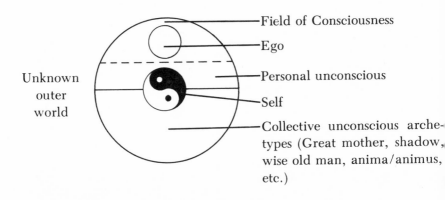

The *Ego* is the small circle floating in its field of consciousness in the upper portion of the diagram. Ego is what I experience as *me* and think of as *I*, the part that wills and chooses. The surrounding field is everything that I am aware of—my friends, people that I dislike, neutral bits of knowledge like mathematics, everything I know. What I am not aware of is either outside the large circle (the unknown outer world) or inside, under my consciousness (the unknown inner world).

This diagram shows that conscious awareness of a friend or of a fact is part of all that I am and is different from your consciousness of that same friend or fact. This fits easily with the Gestalt notion that we each perceive selectively in terms of our needs.

The unconscious has two segments, the personal and the collective. The personal unconscious contains both content that can be produced voluntarily (e.g., I can remember what I had for dinner last night and my mother's maiden name when you ask though I am not consciously aware of these items before you ask) and content that cannot be produced voluntarily (but which was once in my experience).*

The other major section of the unconscious, and by far the larger, is the collective. This is represented in the lower half of the diagram. Its content is not personally acquired but is inborn. It has contents and modes of behavior that are more or less the same everywhere and in all individuals. It is, in other words, identical in all men and constitutes a common psychic substrata which is present in every one of us.†

The contents of the collective unconscious are known as the *archetypes*. These are universal images that have existed since the remotest time. Throughout the ages men have tried to express some of their experience of these inner perceptions and events usually in the form of tribal lore, myths, and fairy tales.

---

*The neurosurgeon Wilder Penfield demonstrated in brain surgery that sections of the brain can be stimulated and the person consciously reexperiences an early memory complete in all sensory detail. All that we have ever experienced seems to be recorded somewhere in our physical being. The patients and students of Ida Rolf, who use a form of deep restructuring massage and the people who use body therapies like Alex Lowen's *Bioenergetics* know that working with certain muscles and tissues releases a flood of feelings that were once associated with traumatic events and physically experienced in that section of the body. They left their mark in ongoing constriction of the muscle or tissue.

†Here too, there seems to be evidence developing that the collective unconscious has probably specific rooted connections in our bodies. Robert Ornstein in the *Psychology of Consciousness* described two major modes of consciousness, one analytic, the other holistic; one rational, the other intuitive. In neurophysiological research these are tied to differences in functioning associated with the left and right hemispheres of the brain. The left hemisphere which controls the right side of the body is concerned with verbal skills, logical analysis, concepts, etc.; the right hemisphere seems to have more to do with intuitive knowings, perceptions of patterns, space and time sense, and body data. Western modes of education have placed a heavy emphasis on developing the functions of the left hemisphere, the analytic, verbal, linear, and rational. With the introduction of Eastern forms of meditation, more and more people are finding ways to develop the potentialities of the right hemisphere with greater activation of the contents associated with the collective unconscious.

Jung made some unusual connections. He noticed that men in their explanations of natural events or of the mysteries of life tended to express the inner nature of their own psyche e.g., he saw astrology as man taking an outer event, the apparent movement of stars and planets, using it to mirror his own unconscious, the components of character being archetypal forms, projected onto the stars. In the processes of alchemy, he saw the symbolic description of man's purification and growth of consciousness in the apparently insoluble outward problem of transforming a base metal into a priceless element.

For you and me probably the most obvious place to encounter archetypes is in the characters of our dreams. As we work with them, dreams change and assume a more purposeful direction. A particular vocabulary of characters and symbols builds and begins to tap down into a source of meaning beneath the personal level of our lives. To work with dreams means to take these inner characters seriously as aspects of my own personality, to talk with them, and to find out what they are about in me. Some of us do this by writing stories with them, like the myth makers, painting them, or writing dialogues with them.

In Jung's view all symbolic expression or activity has an inner purpose, that of individuation, the growth of a more inclusive sense of self. So the ego part of me has to acknowledge and relate to each of these inner parts or archetypes as they become apparent. Usually the first archetype to appear is the *shadow* which is closely related to the *persona*.

Definitions:

Persona. The workable and successful (sham) personality that we use with most people most of the time to get the work done that needs doing, the socializing, the day to day business of life. It is what people mean when they say "He has a great personality!" A bit like a mask, it starts developing in childhood as the child starts to express those aspects that other people approve, e.g., in America we value personal openness and sociability, material achievement. Gradually individual features and potentialities that are not valued by most people are disguised and repressed—our greediness, envy, jealousy, and the like as well as some potentially creative aspects and interests that were not appreciated and confirmed.

Shadow. The dark side of the personality. Partially it is the residue left by the persona, i.e., its opposite. In the interest of sensibleness and good behavior a lot of imagination and creative ability may have dried up along with spontaneous feeling reactions. The shadow holds the instinctive emotional components of the personality that have been repressed as well as untapped potential which is not available yet to the ego.

Anima and Animus. In a way that is similar to the development of the shadow, we do not identify with our experience of the opposite sex and we repress aspects of us that do not accord with the attributes our own sex is supposed to possess, e.g., a boy should be self confident, assertive, and logical. Qualities which a boy regards as feminine get pushed down and give a particular character to the preexisting archetype of the anima (the inner woman in every man.). For a woman, her repressed masculine qualities similarly color her experience of the animus, the inner man archetype.

There are many more archetypes, the Great Mother, the Trickster, the Eternal Boy, etc., but these are most basic.

Going back now to the diagram of *THE WHOLE PERSON*, the central inner circle represents the archetype of the self. In contrast to the ego (which is what I think of as *me*) the self is very difficult to apprehend rationally but an analogy may help. The difference between a living person and a dead one is that an almost incredible number of biochemical and neuropsychological processes are occurring in that person's body interrelating systems which can be only partially comprehended by science as separate systems. Yet we are aware that this same body also functions as a unit, a single organism, possessing a totality. The ultra microscopic processes in each individual cell are coordinated to the major systems, the circulation of the blood and the reactions of the nervous system. These processes together constitute a unity, the virtual center of which is the self. The continuing control of all partial systems from an invisible center is the most obvious phenomenon which differentiates the living from the nonliving—clearly, my ego, my conscious will and mind does not begin to comprehend, much less direct the complex of tasks to be done.

The self then is clearly something other than ego and deeply involved with the wholeness of the body as well as all psychic processes. In normal old age, as the process of individuation proceeds, the self becomes more dominant and the ego is less in evidence.

The interrelationship of the ego and the self is the drama of personal inner transformation through a process of awakening, dying to oneself and being reborn. What has to die is a kind of hubris, arrogant pride, or inflated ego which ascribes to itself supremacy and autonomy, unaware of potential wholeness without which it is meaningless. This is the essential pitfall of TA with its emphasis on autonomy which leads to power but has no recognized place for selfless love, service, and humility. After a certain stage, potential for growth lies not in the rich powerful aspects of the psyche but in the despised, neglected, inferior parts, the beggar at the gate.

The process of the ego minding and relating to the self is well depicted not only in dreams but also in numbers of fairy tales and myths which therefore hold great interest for Jungian psychologists. Two ways of relating personally to myth have been described in Part 1.

Central to Jungian thought is the notion of identifying opposite elements within the human personality and transforming them into a unity of the individuated person. One further aspect of this is Jung's view of personality types divided primarily on an *extroversion-introversion* basis, i.e., whether the person is oriented primarily towards outer events, other people, and activity, or inwardly more concerned with the developments within his own consciousness. These two types are then further classified according to their characteristic ways of acquiring and using information: the *Intuitive* type looks at large patterns and trends, generalizes, and is oriented toward the future; the *Sensation* type is more here and now, classifies and organizes the details and specifics. The third dichotomy is of characteristic ways of making judgments or evaluations, e.g., the *Thinking* type uses objective outwardly available criteria while the *Feeling* type tends to use inner, more individual values as a basis for judgment of worth.

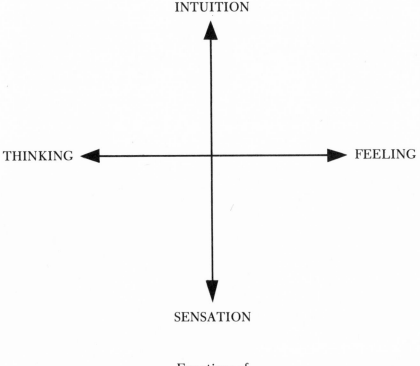

INTUITION

THINKING

FEELING

SENSATION

Functions of
Personality Type of
PERCEPTION AND
JUDGMENT

The unification of opposites means that in recognizing my personality type I have to consciously strengthen my less developed functions. The intuitive thinking person has to take care not to get lost in his ideas but to develop his capacity to work with specific details and heed inner values in forming judgments. The sensation type on the other hand has to take care not to lose sight of the forest for the trees.

The process of individuation is much like a lifelong journey with specific trials and hazards along the way. These involve the confrontation of the opposites. Images of the goal of the journey always represent their successful reconciliation. With each genuine confrontation, something is drawn from the depths of our unconscious nature to aid the ego that a transformation take place.

This is frequently symbolized by the mandala whose essential characteristic is its unification of opposites—the circle and the square, the darkness and the light of the yin-yang symbol. As a symbol of the self it represents bringing together the light forces of the human personality (consciousness, focused energy, masculine purposefulness, rational intellect) with the dark forces (unconsciousness, the symbolic and the intuitive, the feminine). The art experiences involving the mandala explore many of these oppositions and their symbolic reconciliation through relationship to the center.

This synopsis of Jungian thought has tended to emphasize the individual aspects but the interpersonal dimension is worth noting for the archetypes are initially experienced as they are projected outward onto other people, e.g., we tend to select a mate whose characteristics tally with our own inner anima or animus and those aspects that don't tally we tend to ignore or not to see. Similarly we tend to project our own shadow qualities onto a person of the same sex whom we intensely dislike. The Great Mother archetype with her positive and negative qualities of nuturing and devouring forms an aspect of our relationship with our own mothers.

In comparing Jungian thought with Transactional Analysis, we might say that the persona originates in the adaptive Child ego state while the shadow largely corresponds to the repressed natural Child ego state. The archetypes with their positive and negative aspects flavor and modify the Injunctions we receive from our parents. The Jungian ego would be the principle object of attention insofar as TA emphasizes self-awareness and self-responsibility and it would work toward the reconciliation of opposites found in each of the ego states. Although largely functioning through the Adult ego state, the Jungian ego is not coextensive for the sense of *being me* flows through the three states (Parent, Adult and Child). There is no overt recognition in TA of the central archetype of the self nor of the contents and processes of the collective unconscious. TA descriptions of Life Scripts have tended toward a typology of psychopathology but as noted earlier in this book, the myth of the journey of the hero *is* the Script of the self-actualizing person, the goal of TA. The concept of projection is used in both systems of thought and the idea of casting people, trying them out in the role possibilities of our Life Scripts is analogous to the way projection of archetypal contents is developed in Jungian thought.

Jungian depth psychology adds a context, a larger dimension to the struggle for growth and awareness of polarities. Our Western culture, so long emphasizing the rational and technological, has been challenged by a counter-culture in which the feeling side of life and a mystical concern with the timeless inner world are prominent. The contradictions push for a creative resolution in this outer political world even as in the individual. Art can furnish vision, symbols pointing to the possibility of balance and order. They are not wishful dreams but beckoning lights that pull and direct our energies toward still distant goals. As Jung has written, "art, accompanying man on his difficult journey to himself, has always been ahead of him at the goal."

SUGGESTED READINGS

Transactional Analysis

Berne, Eric, *What Do You Say After You Say Hello*. New York: Grove Press, Inc., 1972
————, *Transactional Analysis in Psychotherapy*. New York: Grove Press, Inc., 1961.
————, *The Structure and Dynamics of Organizations and Groups*. New York: Grove Press, Inc., 1963.
Goulding, Robert, "New Directions in Transactional Analysis: Creating and Environment for Redecision and Change" in Kaplan and Sager, eds., *Group and Family Therapy*. New York: Brunner Mazel Inc., 1972.
Harris, Thomas, *I'm O.K. - You're O.K.* New York: Harper and Row, 1967.
James, Muriel, and Jongeward, Dorothy, *Born to Win*. Menlo Park, Calif.: Addison-Wesley, 1971.

Gestalt Therapy

Perls, Fritz, *The Gestalt Approach*. Palo Alto, Calif.: Science and Behavior Books, 1973.
————, *Gestalt Therapy Verbatim*. Lafayette, Calif.: Real People Press, 1969.
Fagan, Joan, and Shepard, Irma Lee, eds., *Gestalt Therapy Now*. Palo Alto, Calif.: Science and Behavior Books, 1970.
Naranjo, Claudio, *The Techniques of Gestalt Therapy*. Berkeley: The SAT Press, 1973.

The Nature of Consciousness—Jungian Theory

Harding, M. Esther, *The "I" and the "Not-I"*. Princeton, N.J.: Princeton University Press, 1971.

_____, *The Way of All Women*. New York: Putnam Sons, 1970.

Jung, Carl G., *Man and His Symbols*. Garden City, N.Y.: Doubleday, 1964.

_____, *Memories, Dreams, Reflections*. New York: Vintage Books, 1961.

_____, *Psyche and Symbol*, Violet de Laszlo, ed. New York: Doubleday, 1958.

Jung, Emma, *Animus and Anima*. New York: Spring Publications, 1969.

Neumann, Erich, *Depth Psychology and a New Ethic*. New York: Harper Torch Books, 1973.

Progoff, Ira, *Depth Psychology and Modern Man*. New York: Julian Press, 1959.

_____, *The Symbolic and the Real*. New York: Julian Press, 1963.

Ulanov, Ann Belford, *The Feminine*. Evanston, Ill.: Northwestern University Press, 1971.

Wickes, Frances, *The Inner World of Childhood*. New York: Mentor, 1968. (New York: Appleton and Co., 1927.)

The Nature of Consciousness as Reflected in Research on the Right and Left Hemispheres of the Brain

Cazzinaga, Michael, *The Bisected Brain*. New York: Appleton-Crofts, 1969–70.

Ornstein, Robert, *The Psychology of Consciousness*. San Francisco: Freeman Press, 1973.

Music and Art in the Growth of Awareness

Anderson, Marianne S., and Savary, Louis M., *Passages: A Guide for Pilgrims of the Mind*. New York: Harper and Row, 1971.

Arguelles, Jose, and Miriam Arguelles, *Mandala.* Berkeley, Ca: Shambala, 1972.

Bonney, Helen L., and Savary, Louis M., *Music and Your Mind: Listening with a New Consciousness.* San Francisco: Harper and Row, 1973.

Klaff, Dora M., *Sandplay: Mirror of a Child's Psyche.* San Francisco: Browser Press, 1971.

Rhyne, Janie, *Gestalt Art Experience.* Monterey, Ca.: Brooks-Cole, 1973.

Stevens, John O., *Awareness.* Orinda, Calif.: Real People Press, 1971.

Various Ways of Journeying

Coudert, Jr, *Advice from a Failure,* New York: Dell, 1965.

Howes, Elizabeth, and Sheila Moon, *Man the Choice Maker.* Middletown, Conn.: Wesleyan Press, 1973.

Kopp, Sheldon B., *Guru: Metaphors from a Psychotherapist.* Palo Alto, Calif.: Science and Behavior Books, 1971.

Moon, Sheila, *A Magic Dwells.* Middletown Conn.: Wesleyan Press, 1970.

Von Ditfurth, Holmar, *Children of the Cosmos.* New York: Atheneum Press, 1974.

INDEX

OTHER BOOKS OF INTEREST FROM
CELESTIAL ARTS

THE ESSENCE OF ALAN WATTS. The basic philosophy of Alan Watts in nine illustrated volumes. Now available:

GOD. 64 pages, paper, $3.95

MEDITATION. 64 pages, paper, $3.95

WILL I THINK OF YOU. Leonard Nimoy's warm and compelling sequel to You & I. 96 pages, paper, $3.95

THE HUMANNESS OF YOU, Vol. I & Vol. II. Walt Rinder's philosophy rendered in his own words and photographs. Each: 64 pages, paper, $2.95.

MY DEAREST FRIEND. The compassion and sensitivity that marked Walt Rinder's previous works are displayed again in this beautiful new volume. 64 pages, paper, $2.95.

ONLY ONE TODAY. Walt Rinder's widely acclaimed style is again apparent in this beautifully illustrated poem. 64 pages, paper, $2.95

THE HEALING MIND by Dr. Irving Oyle. A noted physician describes what is known about the mysterious ability of the mind to heal the body. 128 pages, cloth, $7.95; paper, $4.95.

I WANT TO BE USED not abused by Ed Branch. How to adapt to the demands of others and gain more pleasure from relationships. 80 pages, paper, $2.95.

INWARD JOURNEY Art and Psychotherapy For You by Margaret Keyes. A therapist demonstrates how anyone can use art as a healing device. 128 pages, paper, $4.95.

PLEASE TRUST ME by James Vaughan. A simple, illustrated book of poetry about the quality too often lacking in our experiences—Trust. 64 pages, paper, $2.95.

LOVE IS AN ATTITUDE. The world-famous book of poetry and photographs by Walter Rinder. 128 pages, cloth, $7.95; paper, $3.95.

THIS TIME CALLED LIFE. Poetry and photography by Walter Rinder. 160 pages, cloth, $7.95; paper, $3.95.

SPECTRUM OF LOVE. Walter Rinder's remarkable love poem with magnificently enhancing drawings by David Mitchell. 64 pages, cloth, $7.95; paper, $2.95.

GROWING TOGETHER. George and Donni Betts' poetry with photographs by Robert Scales. 128 pages, paper, $3.95.

VISIONS OF YOU. Poems by George Betts, with photographs by Robert Scales. 128 pages, paper, $3.95.

MY GIFT TO YOU. New poems by George Betts, with photographs by Robert Scales. 128 pages, paper, $3.95.

YOU & I. Leonard Nimoy, the distinguished actor, blends his poetry and photography into a beautiful love story. 128 pages, cloth, $7.95; paper, $3.95.

I AM. Concepts of awareness in poetic form by Michael Grinder. Illustrated in color by Chantal. 64 pages, paper, $2.95.

GAMES STUDENTS PLAY (And what to do about them.) A study of Transactional Analysis in schools, by Kenneth Ernst. 128 pages, cloth, $7.95; paper, $3.95.

A GUIDE FOR SINGLE PARENTS (Transactional Analysis for People in Crisis.) T.A. for single parents by Kathryn Hallett. 128 pages, cloth, $7.95; paper, $3.95.

THE PASSIONATE MIND (A Manual for Living Creatively with One's Self.) Guidance and understanding from Joel Kramer. 128 pages, paper, $3.95.

Cover design by Marek A. Majewski